PRAISE FOR

Letters Across the Pacific

Author April Martin Beltz's new book deals with the letters exchanged between her parents from 1942 to 1953. The letters capture a period in US history when life happened without internet, social media or cellphones. The hopes, fears, sadness and longings expressed in them were just as valid then as now but shared in a more discreet and eloquent way. Meticulously researched and well written, this book throws light on life in the Pacific theatre of war, as well as the home front and the sacrifices that were made to keep us free."

Nora Curran, Author of Tapestry of a Life

April Martin Beltz brings this story to life as she weaves her parents' war-time correspondence with the challenging world of the times. A story of a young couple who each experienced sacrifice, longing and loyalty to serve. It is a true testament to the "Best Generation of Our Nation".

Susan Bodinet, Author of "Dangerous Secret"

April Martin Beltz pays tribute to her parents by publishing their love letters interspersed with actual world events in the Pacific Theater and on the home front between 1942 to 1953. Her father, Bob, would become a hero as an aviator, while her mother, Mariellen, was a hero at home alone, raising babies, and figuring how to make ends meet. This book is filled with photos showing the details of wartime.

Linda Payne Smith
Author "Tin Tubs and Hollyhocks"
Grossmont Adult School Creative Writing Teacher

This book took me back to memories of my father and what the Korean war was like for him. It brought me to tears and it brought me to a sense of awe for the ability of two people to maintain a connection of love and strength for one another during such a time of tragedy and deep uncertainty. I stand here saluting you for honoring the people who have contributed so much for their country. You have represented them in the light of love and deep respect.

Gail Beauregard
Author and daughter of a Veteran

Letters Across The Pacific

A Love Story in The Time of War

April Martin Beltz

Paperback ISBN: 978-1-64719-008-8
Hardcover ISBN: 978-1-64719-009-5

Published by BookLocker.com, Inc., St. Petersburg, Florida.

Printed on acid-free paper.

BookLocker.com, Inc.
2020

First Edition

Dedicated to my parents, Bob and Mariellen,

along with all the men and women who have bravely and

courageously navigated their way through war time.

A true testament to "The Greatest Generation"

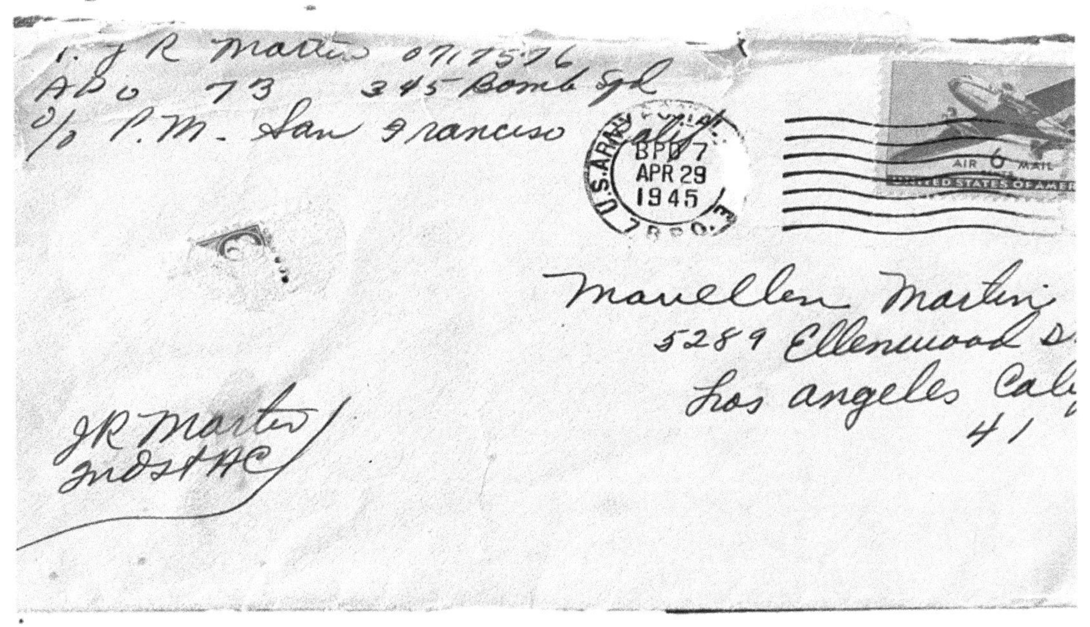

Acknowledgments

I could never have told this story were it not for these letters. So first and foremost, I have to acknowledge my parents.

Next, I have to thank all my siblings for their support and contributions. Though Katy, Jack and I were not even born when these events took place, we all lived them growing up. Julie and Jimmy and Rose provided a lot of insight and I know my dear sister Terry guided my hand from Heaven.

A great debt of gratitude to my husband, Biff, for his understanding and encouragement. This project took a full two years and he supported me the whole way.

To my own five children who read, critiqued, edited, and formatted. They helped with content and kept it logical and on topic. Thank you so, so much!

Of course, I need to thank Emily Holman for editing all 397 grammar and punctuation errors.

And to Claudine Jones and Leslie Burnham who read the first draft and encouraged me to continue.

My writing class was supportive from the start and made many great suggestions which turned the writing into a story. I could not have written it without them.

And lastly, to my niece Lara. It was because of her suggestion one afternoon at Folly Beach that I even considered the project. She was right. We can all benefit from reading these time capsules in letters.

Thank you ALL!
April

Table of Contents

Introduction

Letters connect to form words. Words combine to produce sentences. Sentences strung together become paragraphs, and paragraphs written down tell us stories. Stories are told, re-told, shared, analyzed, and enjoyed. Some of the best and most truthful stories come from letters: letters between lovers or spouses-- love letters.

Love letters from home, wherever home may be, are a connection to the past, the present, and the future. The contents, often uncertain, are read with anticipation and apprehension. They are reread with love and affection, memorized, and pondered. Trust must abound on both ends. Trust that truths are being told with no hidden messages between the lines. How much does the writer tell? Do you talk of hurt, anger, frustration? Or must you be the portal of strength, love, and support? I guess the answer is both. And that is what a love letter becomes, a link to truth, dreams, and hope. And so it is with my parents' story. It takes place during World War II and the Korean War years, between 1942 to 1953 when letters were the universal and almost exclusive form of communication.

Growing up, we all knew these letters existed. My siblings and I thought they were too sentimental and intimate to read. We just weren't interested. It wasn't until my mom passed away, and I was going through her things, that I rediscovered them. Then, I was thrilled to find something of my parents from the past-- especially something so personal. Their letters to each other revealed conversations between two people in love-- during wartime. Soon, separated by oceans and time, their conversations changed, and their personalities developed.

My mother, Mariellen, and my father, James Robert (Bob), met in 1942 and fell completely and totally in love. They married before my dad was shipped overseas to the South Pacific during World War ll.

For the next two decades and two wars, they navigated much of their lives through letters. They had a strong marriage, the kind born of resilience, tolerance, and acceptance. They went on to have seven children and survived multiple moves. Their letters survived as well. Here is the story of their life in the war years, through their eyes and through their words.

****

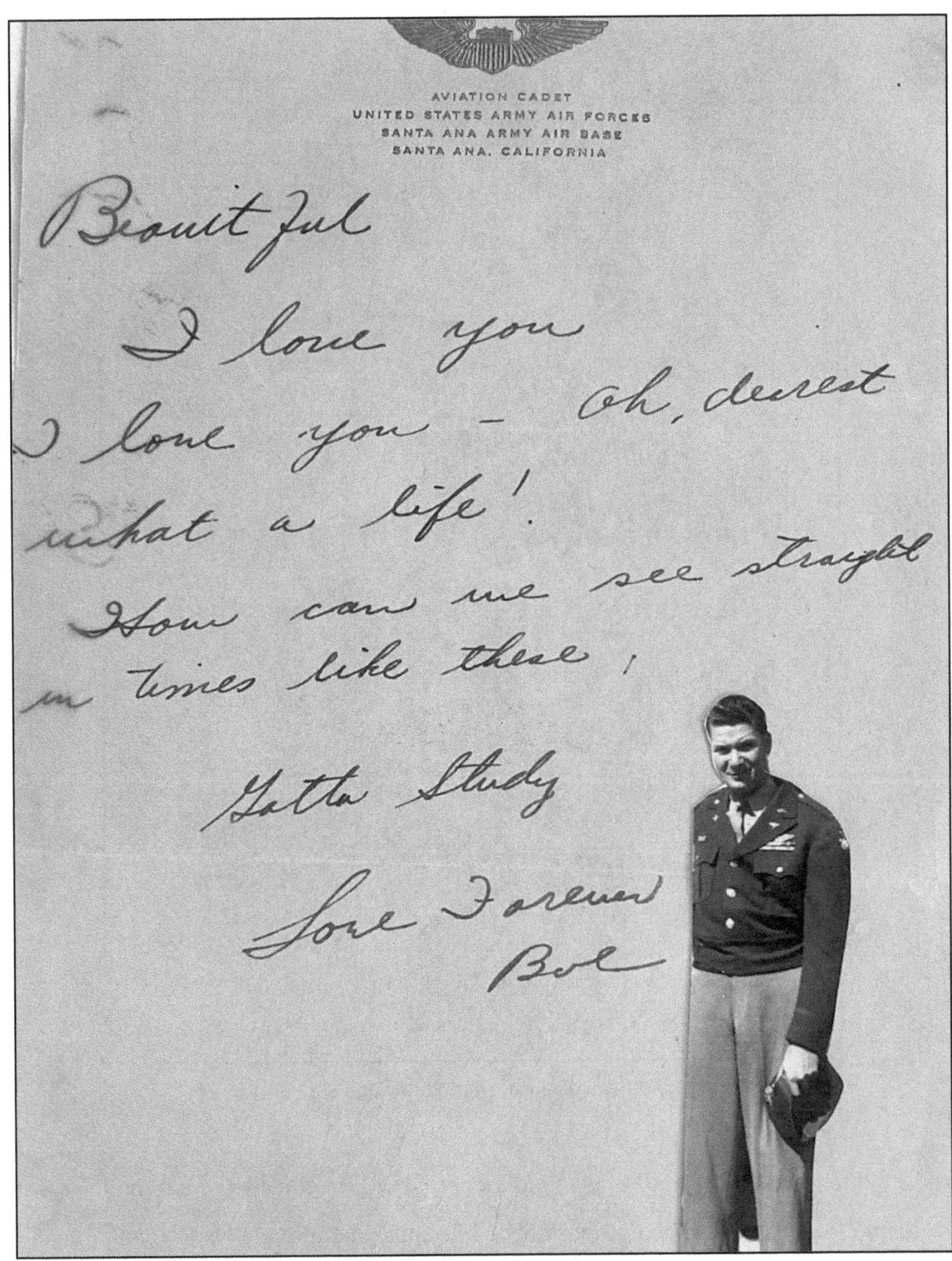

AVIATION CADET
UNITED STATES ARMY AIR FORCES
SANTA ANA ARMY AIR BASE
SANTA ANA, CALIFORNIA

Beautiful

I love you
I love you – oh, dearest
what a life!
How can we see straight
in times like these!

Gotta Study

Love Forever
Bob

Letter to Mariellen from Bob – Shown here as an Aviation Cadet in Santa Ana, California

Letter from Mariellen to Bob – Sealed with a kiss

First-person narratives, as in letters or diaries, are considered among the most valuable sources of historical importance. They provide intimate or personal details, thoughts, emotions, and experiences. These firsthand accounts offer a look into everyday life from home, in training, in the field, and in combat.

Author's Note

NOTE: While seeing and reading my parent's letters in the original form is important, the handwritten accounts cover pages and pages. Many do not copy well. For the sake of this story, I will most often transcribe them, while keeping true to the original content and exact wording. I will keep all grammar and punctuation as written also.

Bob's letters to Mariellen will be in **Courier** font.
Mariellen's letters to Bob will be in **Times New Roman** in italic.

NOTE: Tucked among the letters my parents wrote, I also found some journal pages (written around 1965) by my Mom, Mariellen.

Chapter One

During World War ll, mail was the only way family or loved ones at home, could stay in touch with soldiers stationed around the globe. Correspondence offered authentic expressions of the moment— the language of the time, the jargon and military slang. Letters were like time capsules in envelopes. The physical pieces themselves offered much in the way of information. The paper or V-mail stationery they were written on, the handwriting or typeface, the stamps or lack of them, the APO (Army Post Office) addresses, and often even the censors' marks.

Letters from soldiers far from home were treasured and saved, gifts to be held close, read, and reread when separation and loneliness were almost too much to bear. Soldiers were often away so long that the correspondence they exchanged with their families and friends became the only way to maintain those relationships. Many young couples, married or about to be, found it impossible to maintain the intimacy they had once shared.

Wives and loved ones at home wrote about the details of everyday life. Many wrote of school assignments, blackouts, bond drives, rationing, and prayers for the safe return of their loved ones. This was a time when the whole country was bound by a single goal, and our men on active duty were already heroes.

Soldiers were comforted by the fact that life in the states continued to be normal, while their own lives had been altered and changed, as far from the normal they knew. They wanted to have some semblance of control, making sure the rent was paid, and the insurance was taken care of should they not make it home. Their letters told of foreign shores, exotic animals, typhoons, and native populations.

Bob

Bob was born on February 12th, 1920, in Nebraska, and raised in an Irish Catholic home. Black-haired and blue-eyed, he was the oldest of four children. Much of his childhood was spent growing up in Missouri. He was intelligent, clever, and very funny. His mother was both proud of her oldest, yet frustrated by his mischievous ways, as he often led his siblings into trouble. Bob loved to wear any and all hats. He was a natural-born storyteller. His sense of humor and quick wit earned him high marks among friends and colleagues who considered him "the life of the party." If he laughed, everyone laughed. He named all his dogs "Pal" and loved horses. But, most importantly, he yearned for adventure.

1921 **1925**

Bob was in his teens when the family moved to Detroit for his father's work. After graduating from high school in 1938, he enrolled at Wayne State University. He majored in history, with an emphasis in Russian History, which would prove useful later in his military life.

In March of 1942, three months after Pearl Harbor was attacked, Bob enlisted in the Army Air Corps as a cadet. He was 22 years old.

Mariellen

Mariellen was born on February 7th, 1922, in Telluride, Colorado. Her father was a mining engineer and ran some of the largest mines in the county. The area mines provided zinc, lead, copper, silver, gold and other ores. Telluride, famous even then for the bank robbery of Butch Cassidy, is now most often known for its beauty and skiing.

Mariellen grew up the middle child, sandwiched between two brothers, and was known as precocious and daring. She had an independent spirit, and at the age of two, purposefully sneaked out of the house, crossed the railroad tracks, and walked to her favorite bakery. Her family later moved to a small town named Nucla, also in southwestern Colorado. She often recounted episodes of a childhood filled with mischief, adventure, and fun. Mariellen graduated from high school there. She moved to California when she enrolled at UCLA. Always competitive and high achieving, she excelled in English, her major, during her college years.

Mariellen - Two years old (1924)

In June of 1947, Mariellen agreed to go to a USO dance, where she was a hostess. She had no idea that on that night, her life would change forever. Tired from school and work, she was reluctant to go out, but she did. When she walked into the building where the USO dance was held, she saw Bob. *"It was love at first sight."* He was tall, with black hair and deep blue eyes. She thought he was the most handsome man she'd ever seen.

Mariellen later wrote this journal entry about meeting Bob in June 1942:

Last night I was thinking of the war years. WWll that is. I would not want one of my daughters to live through what I did, yet...every moment was crammed with living! Some were fun, some were joyous, some poignant and some unbearably sad.

My part in the action began soon after Pearl Harbor. There seemed to be a need for doing your part. As a college girl at UCLA, my part ended up by my becoming a USO Hostess and joining the Women's Ambulance Corps. The Women's Ambulance Corps didn't lead to much, but the USO bit led to my becoming about as involved in the everyday drama of the war as anyone could have.*

It was Saturday. I had a job with the May Company and just returned home. It was time to do my weekly stint at the California Hotel in Glendale with the USO, but that night I was tired. I picked up the phone and called the lady in charge of the hostesses to tell her I just couldn't make it.

There was real disappointment in her voice when she said, "Oh, Mariellen, we have so many boys here tonight and there is one who particularly wants to meet a blonde."

What could I say? I went and met Bob that night. This was in June 1942. Our romance progressed with all things common to wartime USA. Gasoline rationing, blackout conditions, and thousands of Air Corp men in Los Angeles. Bob and I walked on darkened and semi-darkened streets, played tennis, talked (argued!) about the role of China in the war.

On nights when I went to my Women's Ambulance Corps meetings, other Air Corp men would snicker and salute me because I had three stripes on my sleeve and Bob had only one. Always in the background, whether we talked about it or not, was the all-encompassing war.

***The Women's Ambulance Corps was an organization trained by professional military personnel. The training included first aid procedures, swimming instruction, infantry drill, ambulance driving, mechanics, rifle and pistol practice, gas mask use, chemical warfare, and aviation and parachute skills.**

Chapter Two

1942

Bob and Mariellen - 1942

So began a romance, not uncommon during wartime. Once the United States entered World War II, the urge to get married among young couples rose exponentially. In 1942 alone, 1.8 million weddings took place, 83% higher than ten years before. And two-thirds of those brides were marrying men who were newly enlisted in the military.

The women who met these cadets or young recruits were quick to form a deep bond with them. All these men were moving on to either further training or overseas deployment.

There wasn't a lot of time to court or date, and if you happened to fall in love... well then, you either must commit to marriage or put a relationship on hold until after the war.

There was a feeling of urgency on both sides of the relationship. The soldiers wanted to feel connected to a loved one, receive letters, and have "something" to live for, a reason to come home. These airmen knew from their training that many would not return and wanted to experience all they could. They wanted to live life to the fullest before leaving for overseas.

The importance of a connection to home was often like a lifeline to a soldier. So many hasty decisions were made, and later, often when the men were at their most vulnerable, abruptly changed.

Mariellen, then a junior in college at UCLA, met Bob, a newly enlisted Army Air Cadet, who was stationed in Santa Ana, California. They fell truly and deeply in love. At the beginning of their courtship, they saw each other only on weekends, and then only if Bob was able to get a pass. Phone calls were unpredictable, so letters were written almost daily.

August 20th, 1942
Santa Ana, California

Dear Beautiful,

I fell asleep in class yesterday. The inspector of the area schools happened to stop by and as luck would have it, visited our classroom. I refuse to believe that my snoring led him to the door in hope that some exceptional experiment may be in progress, rather I think it was just happenstance that he wandered in. He seemed very put out about my sleeping. It wouldn't have been so bad for the class if I had fallen asleep in the seat, but when you crawl down beneath the seats on the floor, that's bad.

When he asked me what I attended classes for, I answered truthfully that I found it a good way to catch up on my sleep.

I suppose that when I dig this big hole, they will just want me to put all the dirt back in. They can think of the silliest things for a fellow to do. I also goofed off on retreat tonight. No shine on my shoes. I gotta stand retreat tomorrow. I don't get to take part in calisthenics. That breaks my heart.

Every Spring we used to go fishing in Missouri. Sorta killed two birds with two stones. Used to wash our feet at the same time (I used to find more pairs of socks that way). Anyway, we would get in the middle of the lake, hang our feet over, and when the fish come up for air (sunlight), we would grab an oar and hit them on the head. Used to clean out a lake in no time at all. They tasted funny sometimes however.

Well, I guess there is not much more that I can say, except to tell you how nice you are. How the very moonlight reflects the loveliness of your heart. And the brightness of your eyes is seen in every star. The tinkle of your voice, the sweetness of your smile (the beautiful eyelashes), all that and more I dream of - being with you - and so dreams are but the nightmares of being awake.

'Til trout come in yard lengths.

Love, Bob

Journal entry from Mariellen, reflecting back to 1942 -

"I'm going to marry you," Bob declared the first night we met. Twelve weekends we saw each other and each night together he announced: "I'm going to marry you!"

I don't suppose The Ambassador, or The Biltmore Hotels in Los Angeles had ever before or have since, had their respectability and calmness so invaded. In those early years of the war, every cadet of the 10,000 in Los Angeles, who could wrangle a weekend leave, spent it whooping it up at one of these two places. It was youth and health and laughs and tension from the top of the Biltmore to the bottom on a Saturday night. Host rooms, which were supposed to be doubles, accommodated two or three times that many, some not paid guests.

I remember the Biltmore with warmth because they did not press these matters as they might have. But how could they do otherwise? These future fliers represented the cream of young American manhood. They possessed sharp intelligence, fine physical condition, charm and a sense of humor that has not been equaled since. They were here today and gone tomorrow, and they knew it. They made the most of the time they had.

While visiting my father in Colorado, I received phone calls, flowers and letters from Bob.

August '42
Santa Ana

Beautiful,

I think you looked lovelier today than I've ever seen you look before. Your hair was like golden sunlight that just gleamed and - golly, it was beautiful. Your eyes were bigger than I've ever dreamed of them being - and brightness in proportion. Your skin is fair and clear and smooth enough to be called "photogenic" in the best of Hollywood circles. Your toothpaste smile was tops and, Oh John, that figure - It was really the sweater type*.

Darling, I never knew you had such a wonderful figure.

Yours,
Bob

***The term "sweater type girl" was made popular in the 1940s and 1950s to describe Hollywood actresses like Lana Turner, Jayne Mansfield, and Jane Russell, who adopted the popular fashion of wearing tight, form-fitting sweaters that emphasized the woman's bust line.**

In 1940 the War Department authorized the establishment of the Army Air Corps and enlisted centers for the initial training of recruits. The Air Corps established the first of these centers at Jefferson Barracks, Missouri, where Bob did his basic training. Since the road ahead for most AAF enlistees led toward some specialized technical training, the centers were placed under the jurisdiction of the Air Corps Technical Training Command.

After completing basic training in Missouri in June 1942, Bob was shipped to Santa Ana, California and entered the Air Force Cadet Program. The Aviation Cadet Pilot Training Program was created by the U.S. Army to train its pilots. Candidates had to be between the ages of 19 and 25, athletic, and honest. A minimum of two years of college or three years of a scientific or technical education were required. Cadets were supposed to be unmarried and pledge not to marry during training. The grade of Aviation Cadet was created for pilot candidates and the program was renamed the Aviation Cadet Training Program (AvCad). Cadets were paid $75 a month. The program was expanded in May 1942 to also cover training navigators and bombardiers.

The training was difficult and time consuming. Over forty percent of cadets "washed out" because of physical problems, the inability to master the rigorous academic requirements or because they were killed during training. This left the graduating class only half of what it was at the beginning.

After Bob first completed the Curtiss-Wright Airplane Mechanics school, The next step was the classification class. Here, the cadets were given two to four weeks of extensive psychological tests to determine with greater accuracy their aptitude for aircrew training. They were given mechanical tests and tests which measured their physical reactions and coordination. At the end of these tests, each airman was classified for bombardier, navigator and/or pilot. If they passed that phase, then came nine weeks in Primary Pre-Flight school, consisting of intensive training in discipline and military customs, courtesies and drills. There were also courses in aircraft and naval identification, codes, navigation, meteorology and oxygen in a low-pressure chamber. Academic courses included mathematics, physics, military law, citizenship, national policy, equipment, and armament.

In the fall of 1942, Bob passed the first phase (pre-flight) as a second lieutenant and earned his cadet wings. The process for being selected to the cadet program was rigorous (just half of applications were selected). To graduate was considered an accomplishment in itself.

Of the cadets that entered the program, only one in five passed the physical exam. Following the physical tests were the qualification exams which included vocabulary, reading comprehension, practical judgment, math, contemporary affairs and mechanical ability.

Cadets also had to exhibit dependability, stamina, quick judgment, a “cool head”, and aggressiveness in the air (or simulators). Lastly, the cadets were asked a series of questions about their family history. They were asked about their dating practices and morals.

“We must know that any applicant will develop into the type of man we would like to associate with for the remainder of our military service as brother officers,” an examiner would later account. Only thirty-five percent of cadets passed and received their wings.

On the back of this picture, Bob wrote - "See if you can find me. This was our class. Ten have washed out already. It was taken in front of the pool and administration building (it used to be a nightclub). More washed out this week-- class is getting smaller."

September 1942
Santa Ana

Darling,

The tests are all over now - all over my mind. However, the mental (under various high-sounding names) are finished.

I am not exactly the lowest type of life. But I was certainly disturbed when the examiner kept asking me if I was sure my mother and father were not first cousins. He was just foolin' I'm sure.

We had a private interview this afternoon. They ask you all sorts of stuff and try to straighten you out on a few things. Among other things he asked me if I was engaged. Then if we had been more than friends. I said no. He asked me if I had ever had relations with the opposite sex. Then laughed hard when I told him I was extremely shy. I expected to keep him there all day, but after I had related the obscure affair (a little redhead) he said, "That is sufficient, we just like to know the world is still going around."

You know I hope the day will come when I won't have that on my mind. When I won't think about lots of funny things every time I see a skirt, a pair of gams, or a lovely sweater. I never want to be so far gone that I don't feel the presence of beauty, but I want to just be normal. See 'em and treat 'em just like people. I guess part of it is that everyone I see puts me in mind of you. Your beauty, your loveliness, and your - just you - that makes it pretty hard. I'll never cheat on you. Both Father Closby and the Lt. that was my examiner, were surprised when I said I was going to be faithful.

I must not look the type! But they don't know how worthy I have to be of you. I miss you so very much. I repeat your name several times to myself before I go to bed. Then I blow you a kiss and then to sleep and lovely dreams about horses -

Darling, I'm sorta bad at being a very good liar, but I love you more than to see you get a lemon or - bats in your belfry, baby. I'm throwing a kiss to the stars tonight - let's see you catch it.

Love,

Bob

xxxxxxxox

Bob graduated from Cadet school in the top ten percent of his class. Completing his airplane mechanic classification and preflight training, Bob was sent to Lowry Field in Denver for bombardier school.

Specialized bombardier training in the military did not begin in earnest until after Pearl Harbor. The amount of time allotted to training gradually increased over the course of the war from 12 to 24 weeks. The course was divided into two phases: the ground phase and the air phase. Ground training emphasized the physics and theory behind dropping bombs from an airplane. Air training put the theory into practice and took up almost three quarters of the time. The 18-week course included 425 hours of ground instruction, including time on the A2 trainer, a bombing simulator. After three weeks on the ground, students began training in the air. Over the course of his training, the bombardier dropped between 155 and 200 bombs from various altitudes and conditions. For qualification, he would fly seven bomb runs, four in daytime and three at night, and had to place his bombs within 230 feet of the aim point to be considered qualified.

*****

Talk of their love and the future was at the forefront of all my parent's conversations. With Bob's continued training looming down upon them, they began to speak of marriage.

Bob, a devout Catholic, believed strongly in his faith. After their engagement, Mariellen, who was raised Presbyterian, began to take catechism classes to convert to Catholicism. Religion and politics were topics near and dear to both my parents. My mother spoke often about her willingness to become a Catholic. Her faith would become even more important to her later during the war years she spent at home alone raising children, while my father was overseas. Meanwhile, letters were still being sent almost daily during Bob's time in Cadet School and Mariellen's junior year in college.

Sunday - October 1942
Whittier, Ca.

Dearest –

Hi Bob - believe it or not the sun is shining. At least it's trying to shine. We might go to Chamberlains for dinner tonight. It's a good thing if we do. We haven't any red stamps left until next Monday. We'll have to eat beans, chicken, rabbit and fish until then. Which of the four would you prefer for Saturday? Take your choice, honey.

Andre is on the radio again. He is playing "Tales from Vienna Woods." Did you see that picture, "The Great Waltz?" It was really a beautiful picture - didn't you love hearing all those waltzes? I can hardly contain myself - I just want to waltz and waltz and dance all over. Let's learn to do the old fast waltz - then sometimes we'll go to a masquerade as old-fashioned Viennese and we'll waltz. Okay?

Bob Darling, I love you. Ever since you called, I've had a feeling - sort of an aching inside me - of how terribly much I love you. Time and eternity aren't very important, they are fleeting - it's our love that is important and timeless. Like all love is, I guess.

Oh, it's getting late, darling. I love you - oh Bob I do. Bye darling.

Loads of Love,
Mariellen

Civilians first received ration books— War Ration Book Number One, or the "Sugar Book"— on May 4, 1942. The books were distributed through more than 100,000 schoolteachers, PTA groups, and other volunteers.

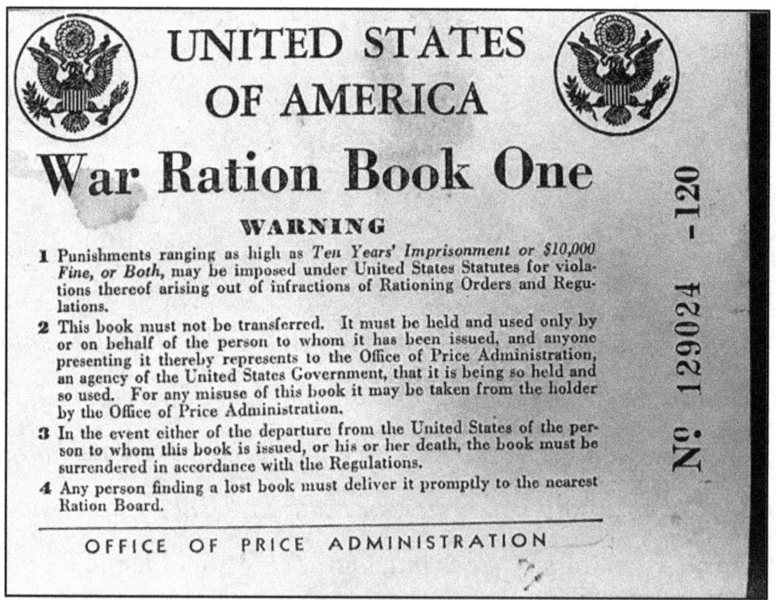
UNITED STATES
OF AMERICA
War Ration Book One
WARNING
1 Punishments ranging as high as *Ten Years' Imprisonment or $10,000 Fine, or Both,* may be imposed under United States Statutes for violations thereof arising out of infractions of Rationing Orders and Regulations.
2 This book must not be transferred. It must be held and used only by or on behalf of the person to whom it has been issued, and anyone presenting it thereby represents to the Office of Price Administration, an agency of the United States Government, that it is being so held and so used. For any misuse of this book it may be taken from the holder by the Office of Price Administration.
3 In the event either of the departure from the United States of the person to whom this book is issued, or his or her death, the book must be surrendered in accordance with the Regulations.
4 Any person finding a lost book must deliver it promptly to the nearest Ration Board.
OFFICE OF PRICE ADMINISTRATION
Nº 129024 -120

Ration Book One

To get classification and rationing stamps, one had to appear before a local War Price and Rationing Board, which reported to the OPA (Office of Price Administration). Each person in a household received a ration book, including babies and small children who qualified for canned milk not available to others.

By the end of 1942, ration coupons were used for coffee, typewriters, gasoline, bicycles, footwear, silk, nylon, fuel oil, stoves, meat, lard, shortening and food oils, cheese, butter, margarine, processed foods (canned, bottled, and frozen), dried fruits, canned milk, firewood and coal, jams, and jellies.

The work of issuing ration books and exchanging used stamps for certificates was handled by some 5,500 local ration boards of mostly volunteer workers selected by local officials. Each ration stamp had a generic drawing of an airplane, gun, tank, aircraft carrier, a stalk of wheat, fruit, etc. and a serial number. Some stamps also had alphabetic lettering. The kind and amount of rationed goods were not specified on most stamps and were not designated until later when local papers published, for example, that beginning on a specific date, one airplane stamp was required, in addition to cash, to buy one pair of shoes. One stamp number 30 was required to buy one pound of sugar. The product amounts changed from time to time, depending on availability. Red stamps were used to ration meat and butter, and blue stamps were used to ration processed foods.

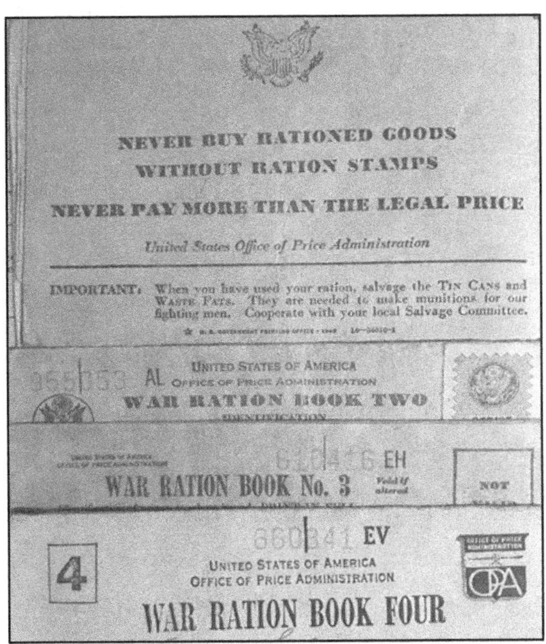

Ration Books - 2 through 4

A national speed limit of 35 miles per hour was imposed to save on fuel and rubber for tires. To receive a gasoline ration card, a person had to certify a need for gasoline and ownership of no more than five tires. All tires in excess of five per driver were confiscated by the government, because of rubber shortages. An "A" sticker on a car was the lowest priority of gasoline rationing and entitled the car owner to 3 to 4 US gallons of gasoline per week. Sugar was the first consumer product rationed, with all sales ending on April 27th, 1942, and resumed on May 5th with a ration of a half-pound per person per week, half of normal consumption.

October 1942
Santa Ana

Darling,

Supposing I didn't start my letters off in a conventional way. Just supposing I said that you were the best-looking girl in the world, not the most beautiful one.

What a liar I would be. But - Oh, well there is no use of me trying to make or keep you guessing. I do think you are the best of the best and I do love you.

Do you think all of our children would look as beautiful and sweet as you (three boys - two girls)? I'll make those dreams come true dearest. With a home and everything. Someday, I'll put you in a palace and make you the queen you really are.

I felt swell after reading your letters. I just sat down to write you a very inspiring repartee when we had to go for chow. Then on the return, I drew up a chair and started again. I got to the first

"I love you" when I got called out on a special detail.

Then at 4 p.m. on my return, I was informed that because of my previous experience, I was chosen for guard duty - 24 hours - That gave me 15 minutes to shave and write you. Then I found out I could get on a later guard. So, I delayed the action and then I decided a call to you would be just the ticket! So I called you - I had this letter half-finished and 2 dollars in change in my pocket. What a mess! I tell you it can't be done. You can't make love to a gal over the phone. First off, it's a pay phone - there are 17,000 fellows waiting outside, eager to get in and get you out. Secondly, the operator - They should all be boiled in oil - and thirdly, I love you. Most every time I get out of the phone booth, I could kick the devil out of myself.

Darling, if I ever see you twice in the same day, I am going to talk your arm off the first time and not say a single word except I love you - the second time. We have so many plans - so many necessary things that have to be discussed - Gee, when are we going to do it? I've got a lot to tell you darling.

I keep thinking about the telephone call - I hate telephones - But I love you. There's lots of things much too sacred for me to say over a telephone and lots of stuff I can't say in a letter. We have to have some long talks, kid. Sensible and grown up talks. Not emotional and kiddish ones.

Do you still look as beautiful as the last time I saw you standing in the moonlight? How can I say I love you, how can I?

Well - dammit I can't put it on paper - I just want to grab you - just hold you close. I love you and well, I want to kiss you just twice as hard as I ever had before and twice as badly.

With all the love in the world,

Bob

P.S. Be it hereby resolved that I shall not rest until every pay phone in this country is turned in for scrap metal and every operator be burned at the stake. And no rest at all until you are in my arms.

(From Mariellen's Journal)

At Christmas (1942), our engagement became official. My ring arrived at our home by special cadet courier, who had been waiting at the Santa Ana Army Air Base Post Office for its arrival. This called for a great celebration! Bob and I, five Cadets plus some of my sorority sisters, went to the Coconut Grove at the Ambassador Hotel that evening.

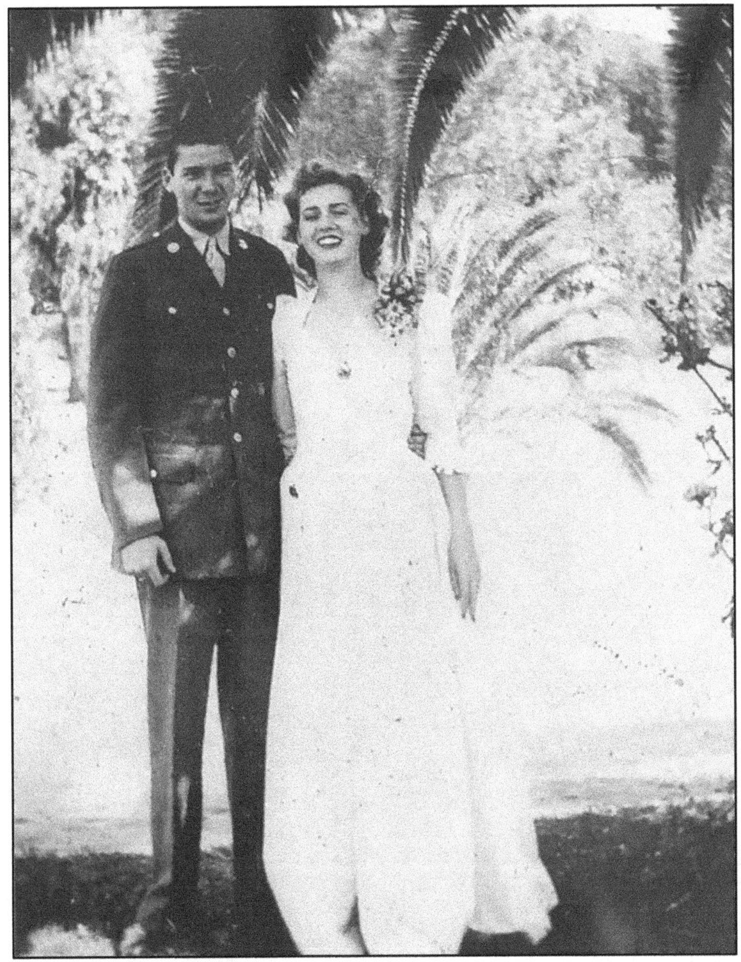

Engagement Photo - December 1942

Bob was being sent to further training, so we decided to marry right away. We had just one month to prepare. Bob's parents lived back east so they really couldn't put much pressure on us to act with more wisdom. My family tried. Finally though, they gave in and said, 'Mariellen must finish college and have no children for at least a year.'

The next two weeks were a flurry of hunting for a wedding gown, finding a dress for my sister who was to be maid of honor, and getting all the things done you do to have a church wedding. I was taking the instructions required to be married in the

Catholic Church because Bob was a Catholic and I wasn't yet. All this while studying for finals.

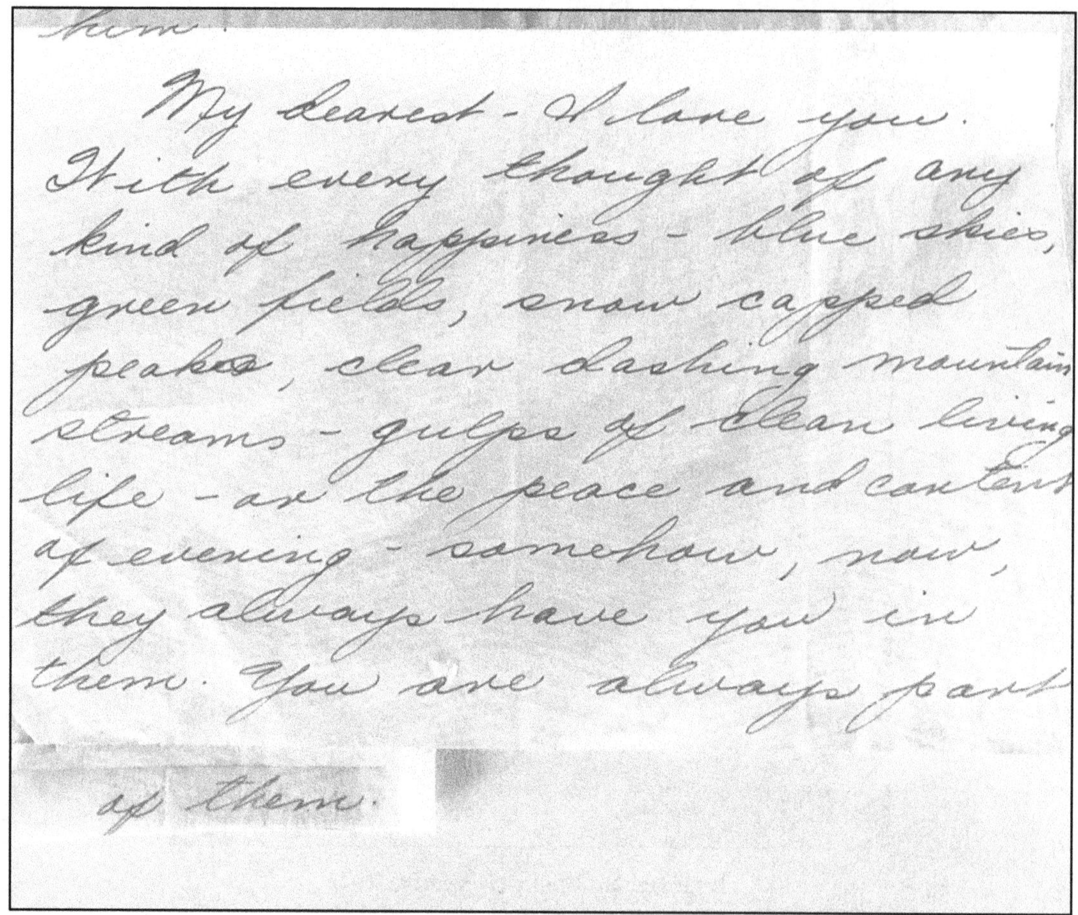

him.

My dearest - I love you. With every thought of any kind of happiness - blue skies, green fields, snow capped peaks, clear dashing mountain streams - gulps of clean living life - or the peace and content of evening - somehow, now, they always have you in them. You are always part of them.

Things didn't go as smoothly as planned for Bob either. Ten days before the wedding, a fellow in Bob's barracks came down with the measles. All the cadets in the building had their leaves canceled for that weekend, with the additional threat that if any more cases were reported, leaves would be canceled the next weekend too. The idea that we would not be married that weekend was unacceptable. Bob was being transferred to a different base for continued training. Somehow, we dared not look beyond that next weekend. It might never happen.

Bob assured me on his nightly telephone call (which he had to stand in line for up to an hour to make), that <u>*no-one*</u> *would be reported with the measles that week.*

Someone did get the measles but with the whole barracks determined to see the wedding take place, the poor cadet was kept in bed, fed orange juice, and answered roll for.

Friday evening before the wedding, Bob called. He said he could get off base the following day only if he was picked up by private transportation, and then not until 10:00 a.m.

*I'd gone down to City Hall to get our marriage license. I found I could apply for it, but they needed Bob's signature too. That gave us two hours to drive the fifty miles of country road. * Okay, I was game... the next morning at 5:00 a.m. my girlfriend and I were up prepared for the drive.*

***The route from Eagle Rock to the base in Santa Ana was, at the time, mostly a dirt road.**

The day never really dawned. It was gray and pouring rain. The road was like a rollercoaster and every dip was a creek. We made it to the base around 9:30. Bob got in the car about forty-five minutes later and we were back on our way to L.A. We arrived at the license bureau at 11:55. It closed at noon. We waited in the car to make sure he made it. He did!

We left him there as he still had to buy the wedding ring. We got back to the sorority house to find my wedding dress pressed and hung in a special room with the train draped over tissue paper. My hair had to be done, the flowers had to be picked up and things had caught up with me. I don't know who took care of the flowers for me, my sister or those for the church. I only know that at 4:45 I had my wedding dress and veil on and my sister had brought a full length white velveteen cloak to keep the rain off. We were ready to go to the church.

The wedding, like everything else in wartime, was made up of bits and pieces. In the vestibule, five minutes before time for the wedding to start, I had a wild, mad desire to run out the door, down the street and far away. What did I know about this cadet I was going to spend the rest of my life with? I had never met <u>any</u> of his family -

never known anyone he had known. Does everyone have this last doubt just before the ceremony?

At that moment someone opened the door to the church itself and I could see Bob, in his dress greens waiting at the altar. I have never seen anyone look so handsome! The next minute I was walking down the aisle to music I had forgotten to arrange for - but someone had. The six ushers knew what to do. Bob knew what to do. My sister knew what to do and we had never had a wedding rehearsal.

Father Bowling relaxed some rules to make it a more beautiful wedding and a more meaningful one. We were married at the altar, something not often done at a mixed marriage at that time. The organist played Ave Maria, not usually played at a wedding, but I had requested it. The whole ceremony was said in English instead of Latin, so that my family would be able to follow what was being said. At the end of the wedding the sun shone briefly as we left the church.

It was the happiest day of my life.

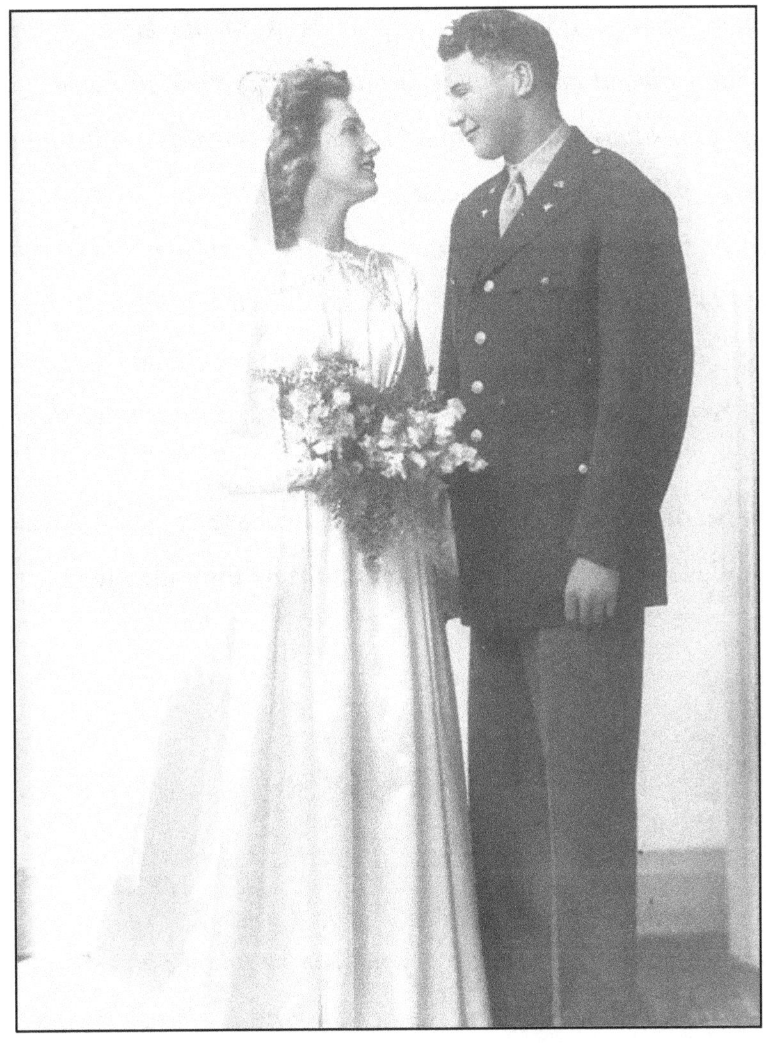

Wedding Photo January 30, 1943

We had no reception. There wasn't time for anything like that. Bob had to be back at the base by Sunday afternoon. That night, after the wedding, we went to a house at the beach. Bob tried to fry an egg the next morning and I almost fell off the chair laughing when he cracked the egg and the yolk fell out on the floor. It was even funnier when he tried to clean it up. He had a quizzical grin and a sense of humor that was new to me.

By two o'clock Sunday, Bob had to report back to the base. At least twice that afternoon, he introduced me as his wife but used my maiden name. Late in the day, Bob had to go to his barracks and I had to leave. I drove fifty-plus miles by myself in the dark. It was a long drive, especially since I got lost. I wandered around in the toughest part of Los Angeles until after midnight. It must have been about this time that I stopped to get a cup of coffee. I was exhausted and afraid I might go to sleep while driving. The coffee shop was a typical truck stop. There were only men there, but they were kind to me, gave me coffee and good directions to get home.

After the wedding weekend, Bob returned to base in Santa Ana, and Mariellen was back at college. They continued to communicate through letters.

February 1943
UCLA

My Darling,

Hi Bobbie dear. Are you tired? Not you! You're too big and strong. But anyway-- I bet you're tired. Bob, it was a good weekend wasn't it? It was such a happy one. You know, darling, we want to have breakfast like we had today every Sunday. I love you!

Forever,
Mariellen

Feb '43
Santa Ana

Dear Beautiful,

Dearest you are perfect. I got my mind off you long enough to type out 43 pages of our 60-page study guide (3 hours) and after checking it over, I found I had written "Mariellen" in 37 times. It was placed in the oddest spots - I always figured my hands were tied to my brain, not my heart. Every time I dream of you - you grow more beautiful - right now I'm dreaming of you 300 years in the future.

Yours with love,
Bob

Chapter Three

1943

In February 1943, following their wedding, Bob received specific cadet orders to report to Rankin Field Flight Training for primary flight training. Rankin Field was located near Tulare, California, about 175 miles north of Los Angeles.

Ted Rankin had been contracted through the War Department to train U.S. Army pilots. At the time, he was president of the Hollywood Motion Picture Pilots Association and a World War One flying ace. "Tex" Rankin, the academy's namesake, was already one of the nation's most famed stunt pilots and flight school instructors when war clouds began gathering around the nation in 1940. After locating an unused airfield in Tulare, The Rankin Aeronautical Academy opened for its first class in April 1941.

Rankin Field trained a total of 10,000 WWII-era cadets, of which more than 8,000 graduated. The skills acquired by these airmen spoke for themselves. The pilots who trained in Tulare earned 6,820 medals for their war efforts.

The cadets, or "dodos" as they were called when they arrived at flight school, were taught on a one-to-one-ratio by a staff of 140 flight instructors. An instructor would be the cadet's personal teacher for the entire nine-week training period. On the ground, cadets had aerobic training and attended aeronautic classes taught by highly qualified civilian professors and experts. The training was rigorous, and the cadets were subjected to a quiz during class almost every day.

The cadets who trained at Rankin Field learned to fly in one of 200 acrobatic Stearman Biplanes. The Stearman Boeing PT-17 biplane served as a military trainer in the 1930s and 1940s for the US Army Air Force, U.S. Navy, and the Royal

Canadian Air Force. A total of 8,584 were built in the United States, and it is one of the most recognized trainer planes of all time.

Post-war, the PT-17 was used for crop dusting, aerobatics, wing-walking and various sport uses. It has also been in the movies seen chasing Cary Grant across a field in *North by Northwest* and was featured in *The Aviator*.

Passing this phase of training (primary flight training), was not only academically and physically tough, but also dangerous. According to the U.S. Army Air Force Statistical Digest, there were 8,256 accidents, 1032 planes were wrecked, and 439 deaths occurred during primary flight training from 1942-1945 across the U.S.

"Class after class has come through these gates full of hope and dreams and determination. Many have left with their hopes and dreams realized. Others have left in disappointment. But ALL have left with their heads held high and with a singleness of purpose-- ultimate victory in this war. *To conquer or die!* This is true. The records of our cadets bear witness. The men yet to pass through these gates will keep alive and foster the tradition, so that next year we will still say: Just a little bigger, just a little better, just a little prouder, just a little surer."
CAPTAIN TILDEN *Rank'n'File (12)*

While at Rankin, Bob made lifelong friends. Friends that he wrote about to Mariellen:

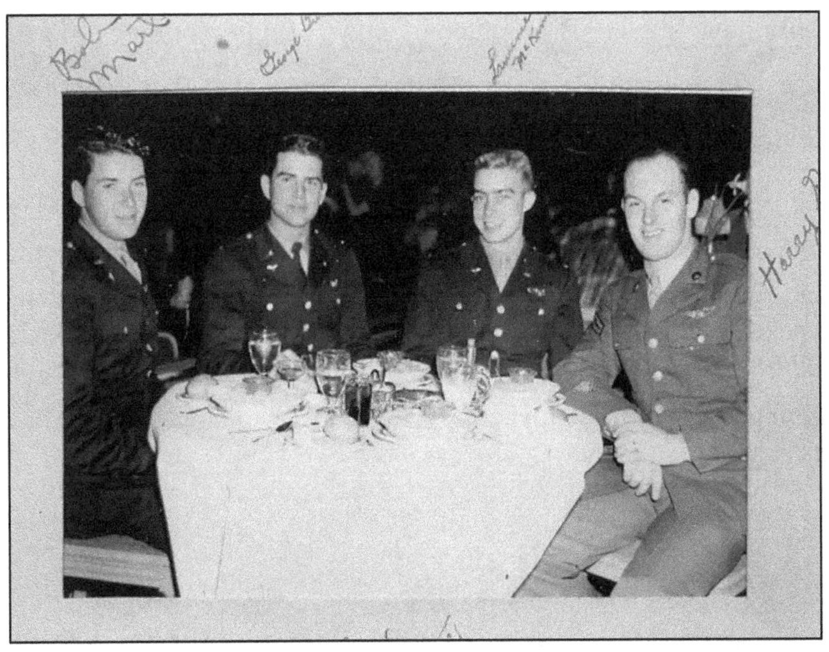

These are "our" first friends. Fellows who worked and lived our struggle with us - who respected and admired the gal from L.A. "Martin's gal." We built part of our world on them - the things they stood for and the loyal and true friendships they gave us.

They will make good, each in his own way - We may well be proud that they are our friends. Let's work and pray that they will be as proud to be our friends.

"In 150 years, America has not relinquished her hold on the torch that eternally does, and forever will, light up the spirits of men and their children's children. America is going to stay American-- that's a promise.... From the class of 43-H" (Rank'n'File 1943).

At the end of April 1943, Bob completed *primary* pilot training, and was to report for further instruction to Ellington Field in Texas. After spending a few days with Mariellen, he was off to Texas.

At Ellington Field, Bob entered *basic* flight training. Cadets received approximately 70 hours in the air over a nine-week period. The goal of basic training school was to make military pilots of those who had learned the fundamentals of flight in primary school. In addition to operating an airplane of greater weight, horsepower, and speed, such as the BT-9 or BT-13, cadets learned how to fly at night, by instruments, in formation and cross-country. Also, for the first time, they operated a plane equipped with a two-way radio and a two-pitch propeller. At this point in a cadet's training, it was decided whether he would go to single-engine or twin-engine advanced flying school.

April 1943
Los Angeles

Oh Darling,

Darling - one week and I'll see you. Oh Hallelujah! Hello, Bob, husband. Hey- I just got a letter from you. You said you wanted me to sleep close to you. Here I am - all rolled over. Put your arms around me Bob. Hold me close to you where I can hear your heartbeat and feel your lips and hear you whisper and know I'm close to you where I belong.

When God gives me that every night, I can live in peace.

love you,
Mariellen

Back in Los Angeles, Mariellen settled in to finish her junior year at UCLA. Then she discovered she was pregnant.

May 1943
Texas

Hi Lovely,

Oh honey, I'm so happy and proud. I wish I could kiss you. I didn't write yesterday - cause I just didn't have a moment. I'll explain. Saturday, we had no flight, but school until late - then I went into town and bought a few things - sent some stuff and came back.

Sunday morning early, we were supposed to fly, but were fogged out - not until we were up and raring to go however. It's not bad enough to get up early, but you have to go to church too. So, to church I went. Then we were to fly at noon. In our element. Two of the fellows, Olson and McCollum had already gone to town so Mossie and I hung around and reported down to the flight line. The echelon commander had one three-man element there and he said one of us could ride with him. So, since Mossie had a date for dinner at his girl's house anyhow, I flew.

We got a late takeoff and the flight was long, so we didn't get back until after dark. The mess hall was closed tighter than a drum and so the Lt. got us out of the gate in his car and took us to town for dinner. We ate at a little place on the edge of town - chicken in the rough and it was good. Then he brought us back - some swell guy. We got back just at lights out. Monday morning, we prepared for our search mission. We flew it Monday afternoon and I was busier than a cat on a tin roof. That was a rugged mission all right.

I love you - I love you and I love you. Beautiful what are you doing now? I've only memories of you and golly they are wonderful.

My life starts with you. I can't think of anything before. My greatest friend, my best pal, my best gal. The most beautiful woman in the world - my wife.

I love you,
Bob

Sunday night - 10 o'clock
Los Angeles

Darling,

It's too late to write a letter - but I just need to write and tell you how much when bedtime comes - how awfully much I want to go to sleep in your arms. With my back to you and your arms around me - I can turn my face against yours and leave it for a minute. Oh darling, I do love you so much.

Goodnight - xxxxoooo
Yours,
Mariellen

In the summer of 1943, Bob was training at Ellington Field in Texas. Mariellen missed him terribly, yet at the same time was very proud of him. They continued to write almost daily, and he tried to phone as often as he could. Meanwhile, in Los Angeles, she was pregnant, worried, and afraid for the future.

The war was real and affected everyone. Congress approved changing the draft age by lowering it to 18 and raising it to 37. Everyone Mariellen knew and loved seemed to be serving their country. Her brother's wife, Thelma, came to stay with her and her parents. She was also pregnant, and her husband, Mariellen's brother Jack, had just been shipped out. The living situation worked out well since everyone could share ration and gasoline cards and chores.

My mom spoke of playing cards with family and friends in the evenings after dinner or gathering around the radio to listen to news or shows. Always, the talk shifted to the war. They dealt with blackouts, brownouts, and civil defense drills. Street lights were switched off or dimmed and shielded to deflect the light downward. Essential lights, such as traffic lights and vehicle headlights, were fitted with slotted covers to deflect their beams toward the ground.

Practice air raids became common in Los Angeles. Sirens announced that homeowners should shut off house lights. Residents put up heavy black curtains to cover the windows. Helmeted air raid wardens wearing armbands walked down the middle of the street, checking that no interior house lights were visible.

Popular songs revolved around the war, such as: *"Praise the Lord and Pass the Ammunition,"* and *"Coming in on a Wing and a Prayer."* Sentimental songs about loneliness and loss were also popular: "*I'll Walk Alone,*" "*I'll Be Seeing You,*" and "*Don't Sit Under The Apple Tree With Anyone Else But Me,*" among many others.

Wartime was a somber time. Homes began to display a "blue star flag." A blue star was sewn on a piece of white, usually satin material with a red border. If there were more than one member serving, the family added stars. Gold Stars were awarded to families that had lost a son, or father.

My mom later talked about her feelings on what she and my dad felt was the unjust internment of Japanese Americans. How fine a line patriotism is. To believe in and support the war effort and our soldiers yet disagree with decisions made by our government.

During World War II, more than 127,000 Japanese-American citizens were imprisoned at internment camps in the United States. Their only crime was that they had Japanese ancestry. The fear was that if the Japanese invaded the West Coast of America, where there was a large Japanese population, they would be loyal to Japan instead of the United States. President Roosevelt signed an executive order (Executive Order 9066) in 1942 that forced all Japanese-Americans into internment camps in America's interior. The majority of those sent to the internment camps had been born in the United States.

Because the camps were not completed when Roosevelt signed the order, the Japanese were housed in temporary shelters such as stables at racetracks. Many of those affected sold their homes and businesses for a fraction of what they were worth because they didn't know if or when they would return.

President Roosevelt rescinded the order in 1944, two years after signing it.

June '43
Texas

Dear Beautiful,

The day is almost half over. We have school this evening and then a shave, shower and bed.

We had stew tonight. And I had twice as much as anyone else. There is just something ordinary about stew. Ol' Irish stew, that is just better than most any other dish. It's a good plain meal and I guess my love of it will separate me forever from the highbrows of New York.

However, my love for you will always be the difference between mere men and the fact that I had the opportunity to see a bit of heaven - and marry her.

I love you,
Bob

In the summer of 1943, Bob, still in Texas, was sent to attend gunnery training in the desert near Las Vegas.

The Las Vegas Army Airfield graduated 600 gunnery students and 215 co-pilots every five weeks at the height of World War II. Students received five weeks of intensive training. Training started on the ground using mounted shotguns. Then they used shotguns mounted on the backs of trucks, which were driven through a course. For the final phase of training, the students went up in the bombers, shooting at targets pulled by other aircraft. Training in Las Vegas also included the "manipulation trainer." The manipulation trainer used 12 towers at heights of 10-40 feet and arranged like a B-29 formation.

Each tower had two noses, two tails, two ring sightings and four blister positions for students to fire camera guns against simulated attacks by PT-13 and PT-17 Stearman biplanes.

The Army chose Las Vegas for gunnery school because of its location. The desert stretched out all around the base making it a perfect fit for practicing with munitions.

Mariellen made plans to take a bus from Los Angeles to Las Vegas to see Bob. They were both looking forward to seeing each other.

July 1943
Los Angeles

Bob Dearest,

Hello honey. Bob, if you get a furlough after gunnery - darling could we spend it together? Ten days would hardly be enough to go see your family - unless you were alone and could go by plane. Wouldn't it be wonderful if we could go up in the mountains and just live together for a week? Do all of our own cooking, go hiking, fishing, dance at night, get up early in the morning when it is cold and crisp - you get up and build the fire - how does that sound, Bobbie? Honeymoon, huh?

Mmmmmm,
Mariellen

WESTERN UNION

VS323 23 NL=GS LASVEGAS NEV 5 1943 AUG 5 PM 9 19

MRS J R MARTIN=

2331 MERTON AVE EAGLEROCK CALIF=

DEAR BEAUTIFUL ARRIVED HERE SAFE AND BROKE NO LUCK AT A
HEAT TERRIFIC BUT LIKE IT SWELL SO FAR LETTER TONIGHT.
LOVE FOREVER=
BOB.

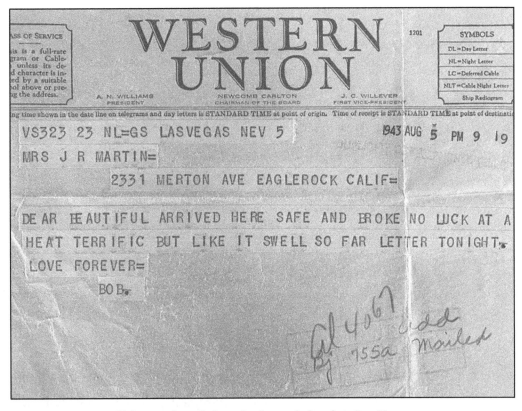

Telegram from Bob saying he made it safe to Las Vegas

August 1943

Los Angeles

Good morning my darling,

And a beautiful morning it is. I am eating breakfast with my left hand and writing this with my right. I couldn't wait to talk to you.

Bob, how much are the rooms a night? I have to know so that I will be sure to bring enough money. Another thing, my bus is supposed to get into Las Vegas at 10:41 a.m. Saturday, but if it is late and doesn't get in until noon, will they hold the room? Oh Bob, two more days! Then there you'll be. As big as life and not a picture sitting on a dressing table. Only two more days and your arms will be there again, and your face will be close.

Bob, I love you.

I can say that now until it will never end. My dearest, I love you. Oh Bob, I can't wait. They say there can be such a thing as too cuddly a wife. Do you think so? Only about eighteen hours until I see you and nine of that I'll sleep. Goodnight precious - mmmm -

It'll seem swell to see a lighted town again. The Las Vegas lights will blind my dimmed-out eyes. It's almost hello again, huh? I love you,

Always Yours,
Mariellen

During war time, husbands often formed new ambitions and emotions based on their military experiences. Wives developed patterns of independence, and both had to adjust psychologically to the separation.

Meeting in Vegas was a morale boost to both my parents. My mom said that being pregnant and with Bob so far away, had infiltrated her confidence. She wasn't sure he would still be attracted to an expectant wife. He was! Starting a family was a way of beginning their life together. My dad had a way of looking beyond the war, when they would be together every day. For my mom it was harder. She was afraid - all the time - for him.

Mariellen took the bus back to Los Angeles and Bob returned to Ellington Field, Texas to begin Navigation training.

September 1943
Ellington Field, Texas

Hi Lovely,

I love you - I tried to call you tonight, but no dice. The only time I can use the phone there is a line as long as a block ahead of me and I can't wait that long.

We spent all morning in a metro lecture on Alaskan weather, then had to do a problem flight of picking out the best route from Seattle to the Bering Sea Base #1(secret)then to the big Japanese aircraft factories (bomb them) and fly on to a base in Russia.

Then this afternoon we spent all the time sitting to a four-hour lecture on how to plot stationary curves. It's kinda Greek to me and all tonight plotting one for the moon and shooting it. We have to be learning the stars now. It's not so bad, but they go roaming all over the sky and you have to hunt for them every night. It's funny learning all this celestial when we still have 8 or 9 missions to fly yet, and that search, R/A and interception is not easy.

I dreamed my grandfather died last night and that's a sure sign of Bobbies coming. I remember that from my dream books. So, I'm trying to help by dreaming him up. I woke up and said I'll tell Mariellen that I dreamed it. Of course, my grandfather is already dead - but it was just a dream. Mostly I dream of you - the golden hair, the soft brown eyes, the lovely figure, the smile, the laugh, the love I have for you and you for me.

Sweetheart, I love you - every second it's more and every time I just know I couldn't love you more - but I do.

I love you. I got a kiss for you. Here'tis - smmmmmack

Bob

Mariellen spent the fall and winter of 1943 in Los Angeles, pregnant and preparing for the baby.

Meanwhile, America's economy performed astonishing feats during World War II. Car manufacturers retooled their plants to produce war goods. Soon, huge new factories built with government and private funds appeared around the nation. Millions of new jobs were created, and millions of Americans moved to new communities to fill them. Annual economic production, as measured by the Gross National Product (GNP), more than doubled between the years 1940-1945, rising from $99.7 billion to nearly $212 billion.

To meet America's metal needs, scrap was salvaged from basements, backyards, and attics. Old cars, bed frames, radiators, pots, and pipes were a few of the items gathered at metal "scrap drives" around the nation. Americans also collected rubber, tin, nylon, and paper to give at salvage drives.

Ammunition for rifles, artillery, mortars, and other weapons was one of the most important manufacturing priorities of World War II. Glycerin was a key ingredient needed to make the explosives in bombs and ammunition. To help, Americans were encouraged to save household waste fat, which was used to make glycerin. The American Fat Salvage Committee was created to urge housewives to save all the excess fat rendered from cooking and donate it to the army to produce explosives. As explained to Minnie Mouse and Pluto in one wartime video, fats are used to make glycerin, and glycerin is used to make things blow up.

Other household goods, including rags, paper, silk, string, and tinfoil, were also recycled. This was a home front project that all Americans could join. Nylon and silk were used for parachutes and other war materials, such as airplane cords and ropes. Tinfoil was used as radar-confusing chaff. The balls of tinfoil were collected and sold to scrap buyers, then were shredded, and the little flakes were dropped from aircraft when they entered enemy airspace. The chaff caused radar-controlled weapons such as the ones the Germans had, to miss their targets and confuse radar operators as to the number of incoming planes.

During World War II, as an alternative to rationing, Americans planted "Victory Gardens," in which they grew some of their own food. By 1945, some 20 million such gardens were in use, and accounted for about 40 percent of all vegetables consumed in the United States. The Victory Program did more than just help to solve an economic problem for the United States during the 1940s. It joined the nation together with social activities and events that helped to raise the spirits of all Americans during troubled times.

My mom often spoke of the Victory Garden she'd planted in Los Angeles during this time. Raised in a farming community in Colorado, growing vegetables was a part of her childhood. She continued to have beautiful gardens, and canned and preserved fruits and vegetables her whole life.

*****

Bob continued navigation training in Texas. The war in Europe was being hard fought and American forces joined the British as the Allies invaded Italy. The 503rd Parachute group under General MacArthur, landed in New Guinea. And still my dad trained. He ultimately trained for 22 months and earned six pairs of wings before being shipped overseas.

Bob - middle back

Of the three positions — pilot, bombardier, and navigator — navigators required the highest aptitude score because of the math skills required. Today when a plane sets off to drop bombs on a target, the pilot punches in the coordinates into their Global Positioning System (GPS) and follows the steering cues on the display panel. But, back in World War II, such technology didn't exist. They used only the classic navigational tools: a map, a compass, and some intuition.

Cadets flew 20 navigation flights, rotating between primary navigators and plotting the course as the training flight progressed. Navigators undertook about 500 hours of ground instruction. Assuming they had ten hours of classes per day, five days a week, that meant ten weeks on the ground followed by another 100 hours of training in the air. To earn their navigator's wings, they needed to navigate with no more than a 1.5-degree course error and no more than 1.5 minutes of error per flight hour. At night, students had to arrive within fifteen miles of their objectives. Emphasis was placed on precision dead-reckoning navigation with basic proficiency in radio and celestial navigation.

The World War II aviation cadet program provided training for navigators, bombardiers, observers, and ground duty specialties, in addition to pilots. Those pilot cadets being groomed for the B-25 had to pass all phases of training, meaning they had to pass training for navigators, bombardiers, observers as well as for pilots. Qualifications for these programs were similar to those for pilot training, though bombardiers and navigators could be slightly shorter or taller—applicants had to be at least 60" and not more than 76" tall for acceptance into the program, provided they passed screening. After taking the preliminary physical and mental exams like other aviation cadet candidates, bombardier applicants were questioned by members of the Examining Board about their loyalty and patriotism because they would be working with highly classified bombsights and other equipment. Stanine or aptitude scores to qualify for bombardier and navigator training remained consistently higher than those needed to qualify for pilot training. An Air Corps paper from early 1942 specified that trainees had to first complete a course in aircraft observation before specializing as either navigators or bombardiers.

At the completion of their programs, graduates would be rated as either Aircraft Observer (Bombardier) or Aircraft Observer (Navigator) and, like their pilot training counterparts, they would be commissioned as second lieutenants. Unlike the shortened length of pilot training, the curriculum was increased from 15 weeks to 18 in April 1943.

Page from the "Astro Compass" publication. The Class of 44-2 Advanced Navigators - Ellington Field, Texas

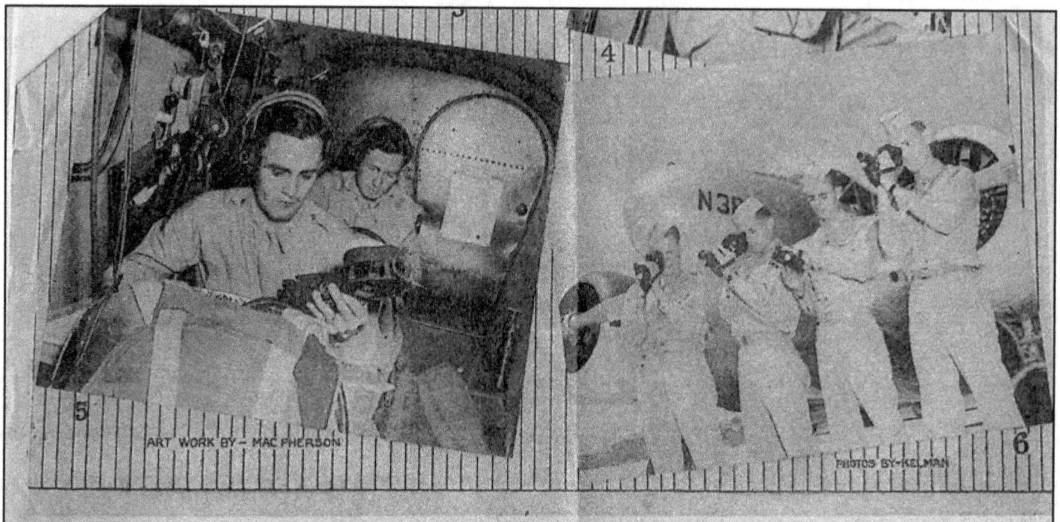

5 ART WORK BY— MAC PHERSON

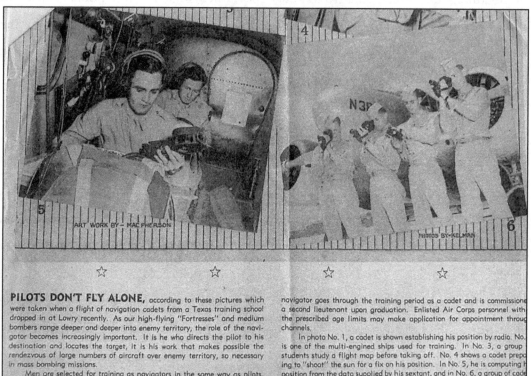

4

6 PHOTOS BY-KELMAN

PILOTS DON'T FLY ALONE, according to these pictures which were taken when a flight of navigation cadets from a Texas training school dropped in at Lowry recently. As our high-flying "Fortresses" and medium bombers range deeper and deeper into enemy territory, the role of the navigator becomes increasingly important. It is he who directs the pilot to his destination and locates the target, it is his work that makes possible the rendezvous of large numbers of aircraft over enemy territory, so necessary in mass bombing missions.

Men are selected for training as navigators in the same way as pilots, though the physical requirements are not quite so exacting. The prospective navigator goes through the training period as a cadet and is commissione a second lieutenant upon graduation. Enlisted Air Corps personnel with the prescribed age limits may make application for appointment throug channels.

In photo No. 1, a cadet is shown establishing his position by radio. No. is one of the multi-engined ships used for training. In No. 3, a group students study a flight map before taking off. No. 4 shows a cadet prepa ing to "shoot" the sun for a fix on his position. In No. 5, he is computing h position from the data supplied by his sextant, and in No. 6, a group of cade practice with sextant.

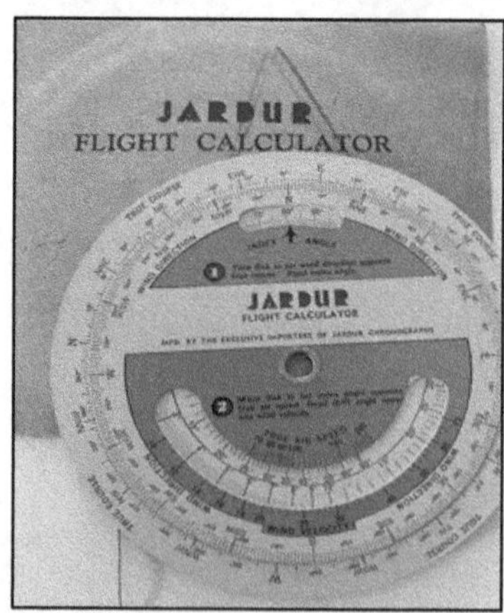

Mariellen was due with their first child at the end of December 1943. She stayed in Los Angeles, close to family, while Bob was still at Ellington Field in Texas, finishing up Advanced Navigation Training. As the holidays approached, they both wished to be together. Mariellen did her best to send positive, supportive notes to Bob.

November 1943
Los Angeles

Hi Bobbie,

Isn't it a grand day? Bob, when I sit down to write to you - sometimes I just sit - sort of with you. We're together inside without anything being said. It's like resting.

I'm loving you and I'm there beside you.

We had fun last night. We had dinner for everyone, then we played blackjack and laughed and laughed. Mrs. Murphy was over and so was Alice. I haven't laughed that much for a long time.

Darling, here's good news for you. You don't have to worry anymore about getting old. In the "Thin Man," Nora Charles says experience is always preferable to youth. Honey, you have both. Just look at what you have accomplished in a year. Last year, an engagement ring - this year a baby basket. Come to think of it the first time you kissed me, darling, you were pretty good. The way you made me feel... Hey - guess what? I love you, Bob.

Honey, it is still pouring rain here. This morning when I went to Mass, it almost drowned me. I still drive the car. I guess I still do everything I ever have done except sports. Honey, don't worry too much if you can't write. Heck, if you can't, you can't.

I love you - forever and ever,
Mariellen

November 1943

Texas

Honey,

It's cold here today. Real cold. We had ice on the streets today and so that's cold. I'm a warm weather man myself - how about you?

I guess Jack is scheduled to leave the U.S. before Xmas from what I hear. I'm expecting a letter from him daily, but haven't had one for some time. It's noon time now and time to go back to school so I'll have to be seein' you - Take care of Bobbie

Forever, I love you,

Bob

Bob's brother Jack, was also in the service. He was a year and a half younger than Bob and trained as a radio operator and gunner. As children, they were good buddies and often partners in crime.

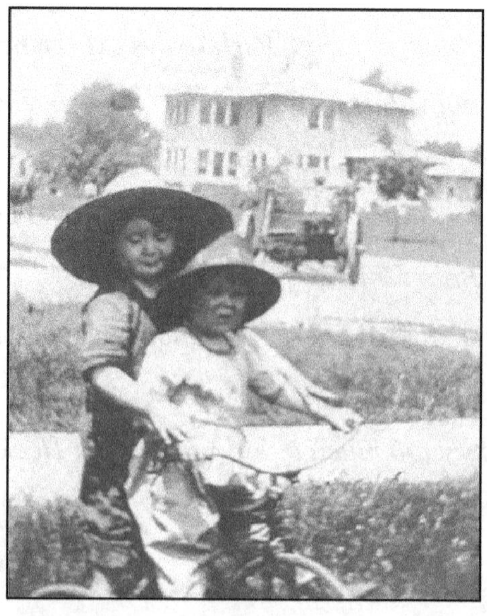

Bob (left) and Jack ages 4 and 2, in 1924

In late November 1943, Jack wrote to Bob and told him about his training missions and his crew. He said they had all the hours they needed and were ready and waiting to be shipped out.

A letter from Bob's brother Jack -

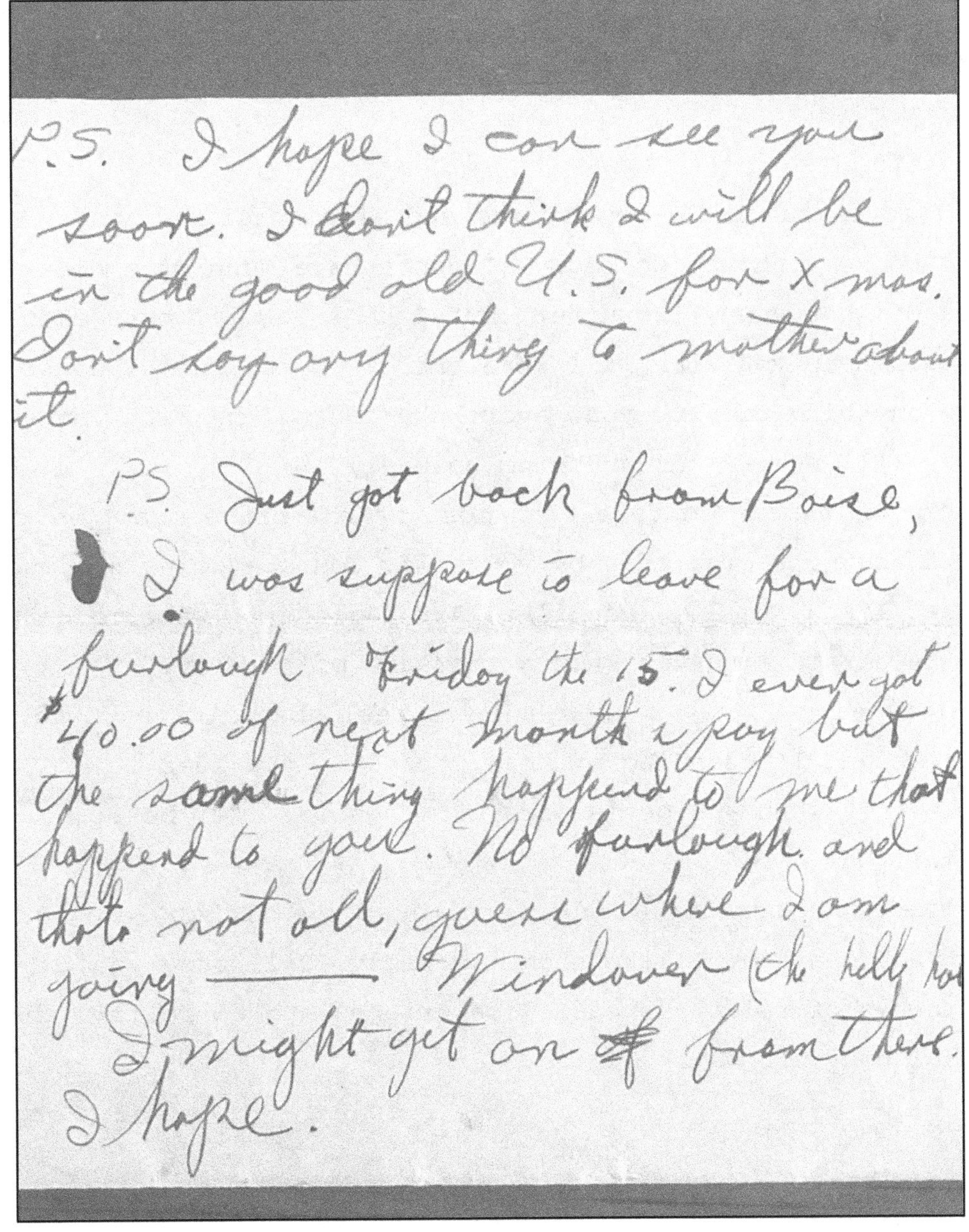

P.S. I hope I can see you soon. I don't think I will be in the good old U.S. for X mas. Don't say any thing to mother about it.

P.S. Just got back from Boise, I was suppose to leave for a furlough Friday the 15. I even got $40.00 of next month's pay but the same thing happend to me that happend to you. No furlough. and that's not all, guess where I am going —— Windover (the hell hole) I might get on from there. I hope.

The last page of Jack's letter to Bob

The Christmas holiday season was upon them and with Mariellen almost due with their baby, Bob clearly wished he could be closer. He was almost done with Navigation training but wasn't able to get a leave to go home during the holidays.

December '43
Texas

Beautiful,

I love you. And I am married and afraid for(me) you - I want to be with you so badly. I don't have much of a clear idea of what you will suffer, but I know it will be something I could help you with if I were there - Beautiful, I don't want anything to hurt you, ever. Why can't I be with you - I guess I'll never want anything so badly.

You have more courage than most of the brave men I've ever heard about. Facing this by yourself. You are doing too much. I feel like I've left you flat. And darling, I want to hurt and be afraid with you, not a thousand miles away.

It's easy to say I know how you feel, but it's hard to believe and I'm sending my heart to you - you keep it and believe it when you get scared or lonesome. I'll be right beside you.

The announcements are perfect. Just the ticket - we sure hit that dead on. I like them immensely. I'll send you addresses of relatives and close friends and to fellows who said I couldn't do it.

Forever,
Bob

December 1943
Los Angeles

Darling,

When we have a long morning together in bed, Bob, will you tell me funny stories? And when we go for walks in the woods - will you? And let's play, shall we? We can play and play. We can go to the beach and play hide and seek in the caves - I promise to let you catch me. I love you, Bob.

Hey darling, sweetheart, dearest - I want and need you. I don't really worry - I just need you to share it-I hate seeing people get involved in little worries instead of doing what they can about it.

Well, I'm getting some of my clothes ready to wear again. It sure is fun, gee, honey it will be fun to put them on again. It will feel like a fresh breath of air. Bobbie isn't really that big, but I'm getting tired of carrying him where he is.

So, for Christmas presents from us - I'm getting linen handkerchiefs for Daddy and Cloyd. I'm going to monogram them. They are beautiful. They cost $1.29 each. I made Margaret and Mom aprons -

We have a lovely box of stationery for Phyllis, $1.00. We got Sid a subscription to Reader's Digest for $1.50. Then another apron for Thelma and Gina. We have the picture for your folks. How about that? I put the prices in, so you would appreciate my economy, honey. Bob there is something that I wanted to get for you. Gee, darling, I hope you like what I got you. Oh, I hope, I hope.

Bob, the basket is all ready for the baby. The white satin is put in with pink thumbtacks over the padding. There is the mattress with a soft flannel sheet, folded and ready for the baby. Then a blue blanket and a pink blanket with a bunny on it. It is so soft and looks perfect for a little one. I miss you so,

Love,
Mariellen

December 1943
Texas

Honey,

We had class last night, and I was so darn tired and pretty near fell asleep while taking my star fixes. I fell asleep the very second I hit the bed.

This afternoon we get the dope on the second - expanding square - search, and we fly it tomorrow and why. I'm plenty tired right now - yet.

The days go by and I miss you more each second. Dearest, I have no Christmas gift for you. Nothing. But I love you anyhow.

Your letters are wonderful. The only compensating part of this is the fact that you are having a nice time there. I wouldn't want you down here, cause I couldn't give you near the comfort you have there.

But I miss you so. I need to be with you. I so love to get those happy letters, but I still need you.

We just had to fall out for the one drill we have every week. I have five minutes of time left. There's so much I want to write - but I can't just now. I just don't feel it. I can write the things I want when I feel 'em but not now. Just resentment is all I have and when I try to cover it up - it looks tinny.

Precious I love you - Gotta go for now,

Okay, I feel a little better now and I'll add some to the sour note. Christmas songs make me feel sad, glad, happy and lonesome all at once. I keep thinking of my future Christmases. You making fruit cake, candy, and all the Christmas fixins. Me struggling with a tree, and playing with

Bobbie's trains and toys, and singing and playing and warm and nice.

We are going to have snow and a fireplace and a warm couch in front of the fire and you and me. I love you so.

Christmas will be our special time. It was a wonderful kiss that we shared last Christmas eve. Please save it this year for me and give Bobbie another one.

When I'm happy, I can see us together and living the way we want to after the war. I'm not too anxious to be famous, but I do want comfort.

1st- Meals of the best cooking-best cuts of meat.

2nd- Sleep late every morning, 'cept when I go duck hunting or fishing - and stay up late every night.

3rd- At least one cocktail every day week and an "Old Fashioned" every other Saturday.

4th- A swimming pool - at least four horses, gaited and thoroughbred.

5th- Two dogs - 1 Collie, 1 English Bull (for the kid's protection) and 1 German Shepherd in the country.

6th- No cat

7th- One Mariellen-most important of all- I remember your hair tonight, shining in the sunlight, so golden, so soft, so alluring. You are so beautiful.

Honey, Rest Well - I love you
Oh Honey, I loooooovve you,
Bob

Chapter Four

1944

Baby Julieann Martin arrived on January 5th, 1944. Bob wasn't there to see her born, but his brother Jack made it out to see Mariellen and the baby before getting deployed.

By the time Bob got to Los Angeles a week later, Jack was gone, shipped out to the Mediterranean Theatre. Jack was a gunner and radio operator trained to fly with a crew of ten aboard a B-24. He would complete twenty-eight successful missions over the next six months. Once again, the war became personal for Bob and Mariellen.

Though they had talked about having a boy, both parents were overjoyed with their beautiful baby girl. It was a happy time for them despite the war raging on in Europe and the South Pacific.

All too soon, Bob returned to Texas to finish advanced flight training. Mariellen stayed in Los Angeles, praying for her brothers, brother-in-law, and her husband, all of whom were fighting in the war.

February '44
Los Angeles

Bob Darling,

There are so many people here offering to help me. I never knew there were so many nice people. And yet you are the one guy who can let the moon flow in soft silver around my heart and over the world instead of just being a moon - and you're the one person who can put the warmth in the sunlight and take the frozen place out of my insides. I'm going to experiment on God - I think maybe he can help out.

By the way, my darling husband, don't worry about me. You know how much I have. Where would you find a wife who didn't miss her husband? Especially a husband like you - oh darling, darling, I love you.

Forever,
Mariellen

Throughout the war, the Army Air Forces suffered over 6,500 fatal accidents in the continental United States, resulting in the loss of 7,114 airplanes and the death of 15,530 personnel. This was an average of 10 deaths and nearly 40 accidents, both fatal and non-fatal, per day.

Companies such as GM and Packard had never before produced planes or aircraft engines but were given large contracts because they had the manufacturing capacity. Though the retooling and production achievements were impressive, they came at a cost. Airplanes were put into use without proper testing, and in many cases, even when design flaws were known there was little time to investigate and take corrective action. Engine failures and on-board fires were common.

The huge increase in the number of pilots trained, coupled with the operation of tens of thousands of aircraft that had been hurriedly designed and produced, spelled disaster. Totals for the entire war are even more sobering: The United States suffered 52,173 aircrew combat losses. Another 25,844 died in accidents. More than half of these died in the continental U.S. during training and testing.

Many more planes were lost due to pilot error or mechanical failure than were shot down by the enemy.

By 1944, it seemed the entire world was immersed and invested in the war. Men were being shipped out overseas daily, as the war was intensifying on all fronts. In Europe, January 1944, the Red Army entered Poland and the Royal Air Force dropped 2,300 tons of bombs on Berlin.

The Siege of Leningrad ended after 872 days. Soviet forces finally forced the Germans to withdraw and some two million German servicemen died, mostly of starvation and disease.

The cost of gasoline in America was fifteen cents per gallon, and a loaf of bread was ten cents. The average rent for a house was fifty dollars a month. The average annual income was $2,400 per year.

February '44

Texas

Hey Beautiful,

I love you. Now your day sounds good. I'm glad you feel so well.

You know, darling. I have been given many nice things in my life. Things I wanted oh so badly - but the very best and most valuable of all - was the rosary card you sent. I will never receive a more precious or more valuable gift. You're an angel my dearest, and I could never have a better guardian in all my life.

You are in my heart, you are my heart, every beat of it.

The day is just drawing to a close, and someday you and I will be together and watch the sunsets. Days and nights that are missed today will be ours together then - and the more appreciated for the lack of it now.

Yours forever,

Bob

With war comes desperation, devastation, and death. And so much sadness.

By 1944, a serious reality had set in for the wives and families back home. If their spouse made it through training alive, they were faced with the uncertainty of the next assignment. More than 292,000 servicemen were killed in action.

Women were caring for children alone, and many had to join the workforce. This meant leaving over five million children to fend for themselves daily and the rate of juvenile delinquency and truancy rose dramatically.

Along with quick marriages came rising divorce rates as well. In 1941, one in six marriages ended in divorce, and by 1946, that number increased to one in three. The spike in divorce rates had many causes, the most obvious being a lack of foundation.

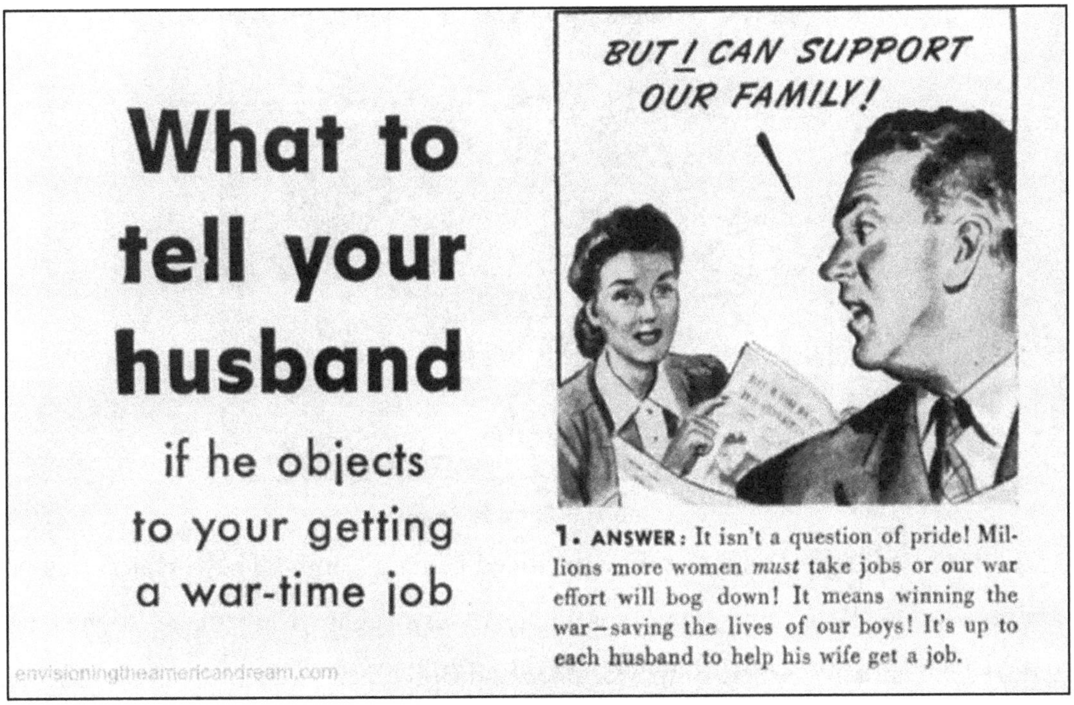

What to tell your husband

if he objects to your getting a war-time job

BUT I CAN SUPPORT OUR FAMILY!

1. ANSWER: It isn't a question of pride! Millions more women *must* take jobs or our war effort will bog down! It means winning the war—saving the lives of our boys! It's up to each husband to help his wife get a job.

Because men were marrying women they barely knew before leaving for war, there was little time to build a relationship. This led to infidelity on both sides. Too often men fell prey to prostitution and women frequently abandoned husbands for lovers they met while their spouses were away. If they managed to stay together until the end of the war, there was oftentimes an estrangement due to the long separation.

At the end of springtime in 1944, Bob was ordered to go to Roswell, New Mexico. While in flight training, he suffered a bout of pneumonia which grounded him for two weeks, and in the hospital for ten days. His unit went on to graduate and he was two weeks behind. This set back was a blessing in disguise. Because he was an honor graduate in Advanced Navigation, the Air Force wanted him to teach Navigation at Roswell Army Airfield in New Mexico.

This time they went as a family. For the first time in their marriage, Bob and Mariellen were able to live together in their own home. These were happy times for them despite what the war was doing to the rest of the world.

Bob and Baby Julieann

Life in Roswell felt normal and they practiced being a family. They created routines and traditions. Bob came home for dinner every night. They made friends and enjoyed the spring weather. Both Mariellen and Bob doted on their daughter. She had several nicknames but the one that seemed to stick was Punko. They dreamed about the future in a World with peace.

All too soon, Bob was assigned to the 499th Bombardment Group and told to report to Columbia, South Carolina. This would be his final post before being assigned overseas. Bob, Mariellen and Julieann left Roswell on June 5th. The very next day would go down in history.

June 6th, 1944 dawned. D-Day. Code name *Operation Overlord*, where more than 156,000 American, British and Canadian troops stormed 50 miles along the heavily fortified coast of France's Normandy region. Involved were 6,039 ships, 2,395 aircraft and 867 gliders that delivered airborne troops. It was the largest seaborne invasion in history.

Allied forces carried out a huge deception campaign in the months before D-Day. They used fake radio transmissions, double agents and created a “phantom army” commanded by American General George Patton to throw Germany off the scent.

The allied invasion was successful, though at a cost. It marked a turning point in war. The toughest fight was at Omaha Beach where approximately 2,400 American Troops were killed, wounded or unaccounted for after the fighting. In total more than 4,000 Allied Troops lost their lives in the D-Day invasion. German casualties have been estimated to be between 4000-9000 killed, wounded or missing. The Allies also captured 200,000 German prisoners of war.

Bob’s younger brother Jack, had been stationed in Italy since January 1944. In early June, Jack wrote he had successfully completed 20 flying missions. He’d just returned to his base in Italy after enjoying a seven-day furlough on the Isle of Capri.

Jack was part of the 461st Bombardier Group and assigned to the *Evil Weevil,* a B-24 Liberator, as a radio operator and gunner. They were consigned to the 15th Air Force airbase at Cerignola, Italy. The *Evil Weevil* assignments were to make long-range strikes into German-held territory in Northern Italy, France, Austria, Czechoslovakia and Romania. On the crew's 20th mission, the *Evil Weevil* absorbed so much damage from German anti-aircraft that they barely made it back to base. The plane was then permanently grounded.

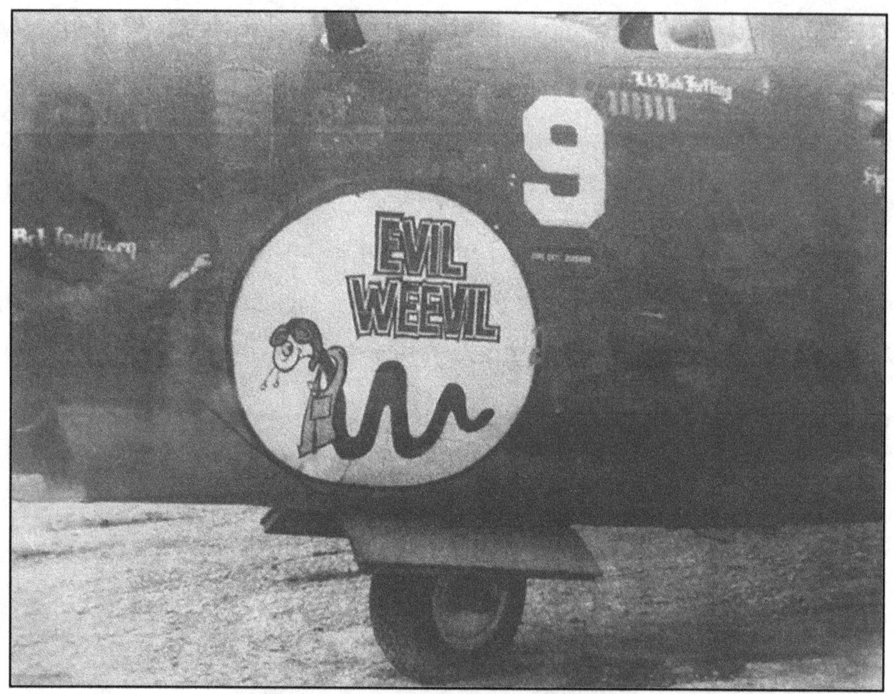

The *Evil Weevil* B-24 Liberator

Jack's crew was assigned a new plane that they christened the *Chippie Doll.* On their 21st mission, the first in their new plane, they never arrived over their target. The intended destination was the Ploiesti Oil Complex in Romania, 1500 miles from their base. This was Nazi Germany's principal source of oil, and a frequent target of bombing from the Allies.

The B-24 Liberators were often called "Flying Coffins" because they were relatively difficult to fly and had poor low-speed performance. The controls were "*stiff and heavy.*" The B-24 was a heavy bomber that held a crew of ten. It was also very vulnerable to the devastating effects of flak, due to the lower altitude it flew.

The fateful date was June 11, 1944. The flight turned into a nightmare. Jack's plane was attacked by enemy fire and before reaching their mark, pilot Lt. R.J. Hefling had to turn back. With only one functioning engine, *Chippie Doll* was doomed. Too soon, Lt. Hefling gave the order to bail out as the airplane lost its last engine over the Serbian Alps.

The crew of the *Chippie Doll* - Jack, top right

On June 24th, 1944, Jack's parents were sent this telegram.

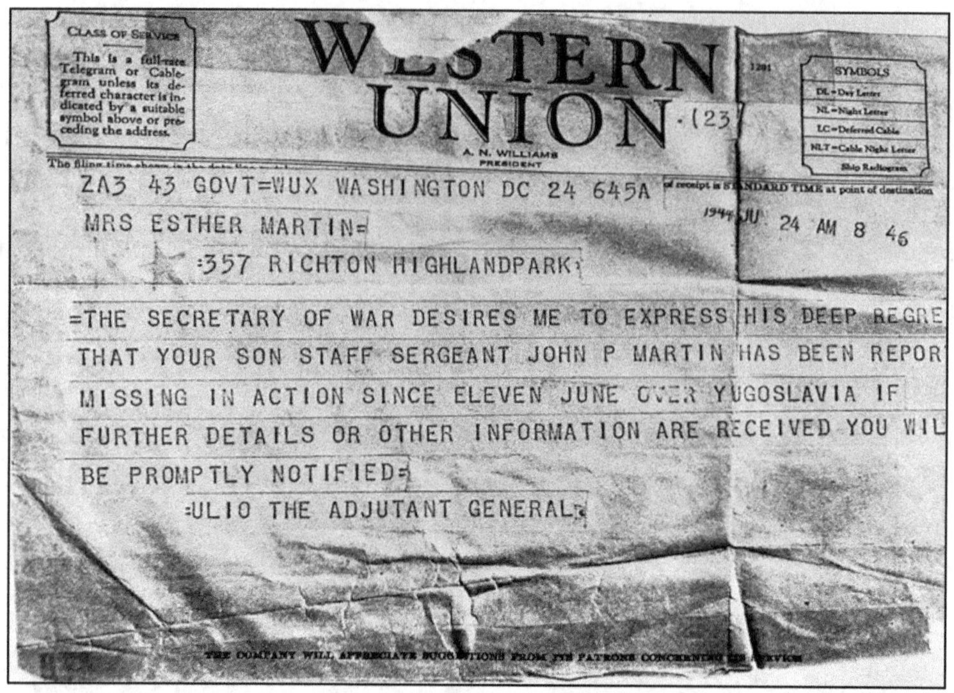

CLASS OF SERVICE
This is a full-rate Telegram or Cable-gram unless its deferred character is indicated by a suitable symbol above or preceding the address.

WESTERN UNION

A. N. WILLIAMS PRESIDENT

SYMBOLS
DL=Day Letter
NL=Night Letter
LC=Deferred Cable
NLT=Cable Night Letter
Ship Radiogram

ZA3 43 GOVT=WUX WASHINGTON DC 24 645A

1944 JU 24 AM 8 46

MRS ESTHER MARTIN=

:357 RICHTON HIGHLANDPARK

=THE SECRETARY OF WAR DESIRES ME TO EXPRESS HIS DEEP REGRE
THAT YOUR SON STAFF SERGEANT JOHN P MARTIN HAS BEEN REPOR
MISSING IN ACTION SINCE ELEVEN JUNE OVER YUGOSLAVIA IF
FURTHER DETAILS OR OTHER INFORMATION ARE RECEIVED YOU WIL
BE PROMPTLY NOTIFIED=
:ULIO THE ADJUTANT GENERAL

THE COMPANY WILL APPRECIATE SUGGESTIONS FROM ITS PATRONS CONCERNING ITS SERVICE

Bob and Jack had a younger brother (Bruce) who was just thirteen years old when Jack was shot down. Bruce still remembers that day clearly, though it was 75 years ago.

"I was home with Mother when the first telegram arrived about Jack. Not having received a telegram with two red stars on it before, I opened it and read the news. To say less is impossible, but Mother screamed and broke down in tears. After a bit we called Dad who was in Alabama at work. He of course came home ASAP. After things got settled, Dad returned to Alabama. Mother, Joy and I stayed home and continued to live and worry."*

***Two red stars on a telegram meant missing in action or killed.**

After the crew parachuted out, my Uncle Jack kept a logbook where he recorded the events that transpired after being shot down over Yugoslavia. The logbook was found and held by Military Intelligence at Langley Field, Virginia. Many details were redacted for security reasons, and the diary was later returned to the family.

Entries from Jack's Logbook

June 11, 1944 - Left field early in the morning for [redacted] Before we got I.P (in position) one super charger was out and #4 engine was losing oil. The first of fifteen fighters hit us. We turned right just before the target to keep out of flak. # 1 engine was hit and on fire. We got four fighters during the fight. Three ME 109 (Messerschmitt) and one FW 190 (Focke Wulf). We knew we couldn't get back so we tried to get to the island of [redacted] We threw everything out of the plane that we could, guns etc. # 2 engine ran away so we only had # 3 left. It finally gave out, so out we went. We landed in the mountains. I landed in a tree and had a hard time getting down. I was picked up by [redacted] We all met at a farmhouse except Hefling. He landed about 2 km from the Germans. We stayed that night at a farmhouse.

June 12, 1944 - We got up around 9. Had eggs for breakfast, laid around waiting for Father* to come. So the day passed.

June 13, 1944 - Still at the farm house. People are very nice. Father* came this afternoon with a lot of news and a big story.

June 14, 1944 - Still at the farm. Doc fixed my head. I knocked myself out when I left the plane.

June 15, 1944 - Getting pretty tired sitting around doing nothing - want to get going - the people know what is best I guess.

***Father refers to the head of the resistance**

June 16, 1944 - Still at the farm but they say we will leave tomorrow.

June 17, 1944 - Had a big meal at 9 am and left at 10. Walked about 35 km to

Got there late. Had a big meal and went to a different place to sleep.

June 18, 1944 - Still in We left to see the Big Boy* today but we came back because of rain. Had a good meal that night.

June 19, 1944 - Sat around all day, the people here are sure nice. We have been eating very good. Buckwheat and I have been living together.

June 20, 1944 - We had lunch with the Big Boy, and what a meal. We have met many people who can speak English.

June 21, 1944 - Germans and Pro [pro-Germans] are coming. Had to leave and in a hurry. We took to the hills, and we also took a bath today for the first time.

June 22, 1944 - Still at a farm in the hills. Food not so good.

June 23, 1944 - Still laying around doing nothing.

June 24, 1944 - We heard gunfire and bombs from the place we just left. Also smoke. I guess it is time to get going. We walked about 20 km today to get away from the Pro. We spent the night at sleeping on the cement floor.

***Big Boy refers to Draza Mikhailovich – Head of the Yugoslavian Resistance**

June 25, 1944 - We picked up a P- 38 pilot today. He was burned pretty bad. That makes 12 of us. At breakfast and the phone rang. The Germans were about a half hour away in the same direction we were going to take. We took to the hills again.

We stopped at a farm house after hearing gunfire in the distance. We were in bed at 8 pm and awake at 10 pm. It seems the Germans are on the way. We walked four hours tonight.

June 26, 1944 – We stayed at a farm house last night. About 2pm we got word to go again. We walked about half an hour and we met about men

Walked about 4 hours and stopped for bread and cheese. We started again at 9pm and walked all night until 3am getting through German lines.

June 27, 1944 – We are used to sleeping on floors now, so we don't mind it. We stayed at this place for the rest of the day.

June 28, 1944 – Left about 10am. Didn't go very far today. We stopped at 11 to eat lunch and didn't get going until 5pm. We all had a very good meal.

June 29, 1944 - We left this place and traveled for about 2 hours and stopped at a schoolhouse where we ate together, the people bringing in food from different houses. We stayed at a very nice place.

June 30, 1944 - We got up early today and did a lot of walking from 6 am to 5 pm with no time out for lunch. We are sleeping at a farmhouse. I slept in the barn again. The weather looked bad for about an hour. We just had the biggest hail stones that I ever saw. They were as big as 2 ½" in diameter. I really feel sorry for all the people around here. Their crops have been ruined.

July 1, 1944 - We got an early start today, stopped about 10:30 for lunch. We crossed a railroad and a road at noon. Three German cars went by just before we crossed. We passed a big town later in the afternoon. Stopped at a farmhouse at 7 pm.

July 2, 1944 - We walked quite a ways today. It was very hot. We didn't get to eat lunch until 4 pm. We were all in by the time we stopped to sleep tonight.

July 3, 1944 - Stayed at a pretty good farm last night. Had a good night's sleep. We went about 5 miles and are resting up for tonight. We traveled several miles tonight and made good time. We stopped at another farm house.

July 4, 1944 - Today is the 4th. Big time in the U.S. We are resting again today. We are on the go again tonight. Went about 25 km. tonight.

July 5, 1944 - It rained all day today. We took off from our last stop at 12. We stopped at 1:00 to eat. This was supposed to be a 3-hour trip but we were still walking at 11 pm. It was raining cats and dogs. If we don't all get colds out of this, it will be a miracle. We still haven't reached our destination. They say between 10 to 15 days and we will be back in Italy. The Germans really destroyed this village. They blew up all the stores and houses and we didn't see any young people in the village.

July 6, 1944 - We finally reached the place we are going to stay for a while. I hope a plane picks us up soon. We split up in 6's. Six at each farm.

July 7, 1944 - It is raining this morning. We ate early at 12 pm. We were told the Germans were coming and we had to move. We walked for about half an hour in the rain and mud. We stopped at a place with 3 other crews and waited. Wilbur gave his shoes to a fellow to fix for him so he was walking barefoot. The Germans finally left so we went on.

July 8, 1944 - Nothing much doing today, Father went to see about making contact by radio. Has not come back yet. Still at [redacted] Farm.

July 9, 1944 - Ate out today. This afternoon we went down to the village and had some vino and tonight some cookies and cakes.

July 10, 1944 - Rained all day. We also walked 3 miles in the rain to a new house. Pop came back at about 7 pm. He said we leave in the morning at 7 am.

July 11, 1944 - Still raining and we have about 5 hours walk to a new village near the L.S. (landing site). We got here about 6:30 pm. I sure hope a plane comes soon. We have been here one month today. I sure wish I were home.

July 12, 1944 - Still sweating out a plane. Moved to a new farm house. Still raining. Bad weather for a plane. Played cards all day.

July 13, 1944 - Still bad weather for a plane. Are staying at the same farmhouse. Two meals a day, still playing cards.

July 14, 1944 - Weather a lot better. Walked to L.S. Not bad, also went to town. Didn't get anything. Came back and played cards, again.

July 15, 1944 - Walked to town today. Bought about $5.00 worth of candy, running short on money. Bugs really ate me up last night.

July 16, 1944 - We got up early today. Thought we would have to move out. We left at 1 pm for town. All night in town. We started out at 4 am. Back in the mountains. We got there at 7 pm. We were told that 150 German Vic were in the valley and looking for us and the L.S. so we started back. We walked on into the night.

July 17, 1944 - Up at 2 am. Stopped at a farm and I slept on the floor for 2 hours. It began to rain, and we walked until 7 am. Had breakfast and went on our way again. We finally reached a village and split up into different homes. Five of us stayed at one house.

July 18, 1944 - We are still at the farmhouse. I don't know how long we will stay here.

July 19, 1944 - Sitting around doing nothing but playing cards. We did some washing.

July 20, 1944 - Thought we were going to move today but plans changed. Still playing cards.

July 21, 1944 - Still doing nothing but laying around.

July 22, 1944 - We worked in the field today. Not much happening- We have been eating pretty good lately.

July 23, 1944 - We were told we were going to move at 5:00 but again it was cancelled. I shaved today for the first time.

July 24, 1944 - We moved today to a small town and then to a village farther west to see the

Big Boy. We slept in a barn tonight

July 25, 1944 - We moved again today. We moved back to where we were about a month ago. We traveled in the dark.

July 26, 1944 - We have found a nice place with nice people for a change. Played cards today.

July 27, 1944 - Went down to the stream today and took a bath and washed some clothes. Father came back today with news of getting out, but I think he is full of bull.

July 28, 1944 - Another day and nothing to do. We went to a big party tonight. Lots to eat and lots of music and dancing.

July 29, 1944 - Washed my clothes. At one o'clock we were told we were going to move again. Of course, it was raining. They also told us a plane was coming the night of the 29th, 30th or 31st. But no plane on the 29th.

July 30 - 44 - We stayed in the airfield from 7 to 2 waiting for a plane to come. No Plane. DM came about 12 [redacted]

July 31 - 44 - Rain all day today and no chance of a Plane tonight. I guess all hope is gone now. DM had a big parade for us with all his soldiers on service.

August 1 - 44 - I have been sleeping on a wooden bench for the last three nights and my back isn't what it used to be. It has been raining for 24 hours. Funny weather for this time of year.

Jack's logbook ends here, on August 1, 1944

Jack was just 22 years old when his plane was shot down near the border between Yugoslavia and Romania, in the area controlled by the Germans.

On April 6th, 1941, Yugoslavia was invaded by the Axis powers in a German-led attack, known as the *April War* or *Operation 25.* The invasion lasted only two weeks. It ended when an armistice was signed on April 17th, 1941, based on the unconditional surrender of the Yugoslav Army. Yugoslavia was then occupied and partitioned by the Axis powers. When Jack and his crew crash-landed on June 11th, 1944, the country was fully occupied by the Germans.

The *Chippie Doll* crew flew their last mission to bomb the Ploiești Oil Complex in Romania, known as "Hitler's gas station." It was a frequent target of the 15th Air Force. The complex supplied 30 to 50 percent of the Third Reich's fuel. These raids, flown in lumbering bombers often with no fighter escort, had several advantages, including evading German radar and precise bomb delivery. The drawbacks? Almost everything else.

From October 1943 to October 1944, the 15th Air Force, based in Italy, conducted about 20,000 combat missions with fighters and bombers. During this time, it lost almost 50 percent of its aircraft, and 10 percent of its personnel.

To carry out these missions, the 15th Air Force had 500 heavy bombers (B-17 Flying Fortresses and B-24 Liberators) and about 100 fighter escorts.

In the spring of 1944, the USAAF intensified the bombing of targets in Bulgaria and Romania, resulting in American aviators being forced to bail out of damaged aircraft over Yugoslavia in increasing numbers. Some crews fell into the hands of Romanian, Bulgarian, Croatian, or German troops and were sent to be prisoners of war camps. By August 1944, 350 bombers had been lost. Many of the crews survived. Some came down in territory held by Marshal Tito's Partisans, while others found refuge in Serbia with Draza Mihailovichs' Chetniks.

Uncle Jack's crew was lucky. They were picked up by Chetniks, the Yugoslavian resistance fighters. There were a few tense moments as they were surrounded by bearded men holding rifles, each wrapped in a bandolier of ammunition. His turret gunner yelled, "American, American!" Immediately his whole crew was embraced with hugs and whiskered kisses.

Mihailovivh was known throughout the military as a brilliant strategist and regarded as a man of great integrity, dignified and humble. My Uncle Jack was fortunate to have been rescued by him.

Mihailovich sent numerous messages to the US Military and Government regarding the downed soldiers. Meanwhile, he began to gather all the airmen in a safe location.

Jack and his crew were rescued on August 10th, 1944, in the largest Allied Airlift Operation (Operation Halyard) to take place behind enemy lines.

In order to make the rescue possible, the Chetniks and the airmen built a landing strip in Pranjane, Yugoslavia, by leveling the ground and clearing trees and rocks from the rugged mountainside. The airstrip had to be built by hand with few tools. Once again, local resistance fighters responded by doing the lion's share of the work, working until their backs ached, and their hands were bloodied and blistered.

All this preparation had to be done in just a week, without alerting the Germans. Only twelve miles away, in the town of Chachak, was a stronghold of 4,500 Nazi troops. Five miles in the other direction were 250 more. In fact, there were German troops in all directions around the proposed landing site.

On the night of August 9, 1944, the first planes arrived on the makeshift landing strip.

Both the landings and take-offs were daunting and dangerous on an airstrip just barely long enough for a plane to land. The C-47 transport planes had to arrive and take off in the dark of night while trying to avoid detection from the Germans. The planes could only pick up twelve men at a time. The rescuers initially thought they were rescuing 100 men and actually hoped that number to be exaggerated. Instead they found 250 American airmen waiting at Pranjane, with more arriving daily. By the time the recovery mission was completed, almost 500 airmen were safely rescued.

*Read The *Forgotten 500* by Gregory Freemen to learn more about these courageous U.S. airmen and the brave Resistance that helped them.

Sadly, after the war, Mihailovich was captured by the Communists. He was tried and convicted of high treason and war crimes by the Communist authorities of the Federal People's Republic of Yugoslavia and executed by firing squad in Belgrade.

Despite an extensive letter-writing campaign and direct lobbying to Washington from the rescued airmen and their families, the United States was unable to influence Tito, the leader of the Communist party in Yugoslavia. These American servicemen stood by their claims that Mihailovich saved their lives. It was he that made it possible for all these men to be able to come back safely.

President Truman, in 1948, did bestow the prestigious *Legion of Merit* posthumously to Draza Mihailovich for his contribution to the Allied victory in Europe. The State Department then insisted that such recognition would antagonize Tito and damage U.S. relations with his Communist government.

Public awareness of the award was suppressed until 2005, when the honor was at last presented to the General's daughter, Gordana Mihailovich.

Several of the rescued airmen and men involved in coordinating the rescue effort flew to Yugoslavia to honor Mihailovich.

Draza Mihailovich

Bruce, Jack's then 13-year-old brother, remembers the telegrams that came after Jack was rescued.

"In August we got a telegram from Jack that he was okay. We notified Dad and no doubt he cried too, again this time for joy and relief."

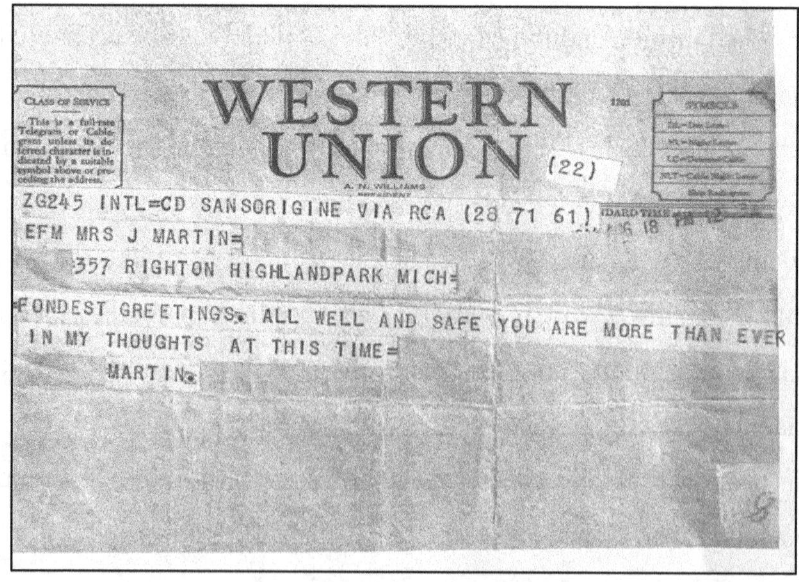

WESTERN UNION (22)

ZG245 INTL=CD SANSORIGINE VIA RCA (28 71 61)

EFM MRS J MARTIN=

357 RIGHTON HIGHLANDPARK MICH=

FONDEST GREETINGS. ALL WELL AND SAFE YOU ARE MORE THAN EVER IN MY THOUGHTS AT THIS TIME=

MARTIN.

Telegram from Jack

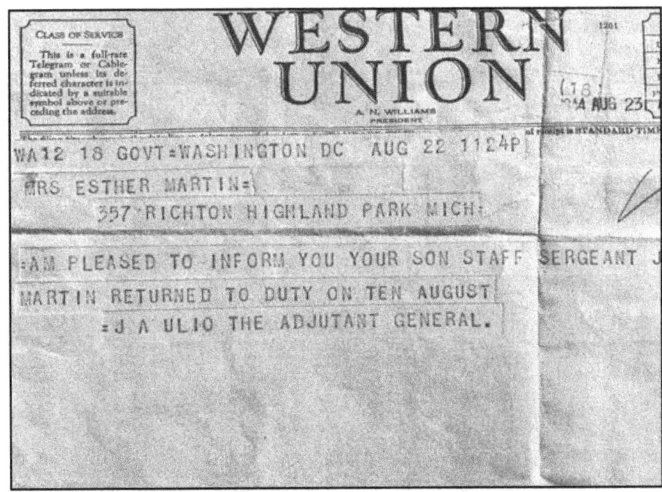

CLASS OF SERVICE
This is a full-rate Telegram or Cablegram unless its deferred character is indicated by a suitable symbol above or preceding the address.

WESTERN UNION

A. N. WILLIAMS
PRESIDENT

1944 AUG 23

WA12 18 GOVT=WASHINGTON DC AUG 22 1124P

MRS ESTHER MARTIN=
357 RICHTON HIGHLAND PARK MICH=

=AM PLEASED TO INFORM YOU YOUR SON STAFF SERGEANT J MARTIN RETURNED TO DUTY ON TEN AUGUST
=J A ULIO THE ADJUTANT GENERAL.

Telegram from Army

After Jack was rescued, he stayed on in Italy and successfully completed twenty more missions. In late October of 1944, with a total of fifty missions under his belt, he came home.

Jack, his crew, and the other rescued airmen, went to the White House in October 1944, to much fanfare and celebration. He received the Air Medal for "A Single Act of Heroism and Meritorious Achievement while Participating in Aerial Flight." He received the Good Conduct Medal for "Exemplary Behavior, Efficiency, and Fidelity." He also

received the Distinguished Flying Cross, Valor Certificate, Purple Heart, Good Conduct Medal, Distinguished Unit Emblem, a Citation of Honor, and a Bronze Star.

Jack was reassigned to Langley Field in Virginia. While at Langley, he trained and tested new aircrews. He was there only two months when, on a training flight, he was killed. The B-24 aircraft crashed just after takeoff.

Younger brother Bruce recalled that fateful day:

"With the Christmas tree up and still shining on December 27th*, we were home when again the telegram with two stars arrived. I read the news and all hell broke loose. Tears, crying and yelling as you can imagine. It so happened that*

Dad was about to leave for the train station to return to Alabama when the news came. Five minutes later and he would have been gone. He called his boss and requested a transfer which was approved. Jack was buried on January 2, 1945. Life never returned as before."

... was killed Wednesday in a plane crash near Langley Field, Va.

The son of Mr. and Mrs. James P. Martin, of 357 Richton, Highland Park, Sgt. Martin served as radioman in a B-24 Liberator. Last June 11 his plane was shot down over Yugoslavia, but he and his entire crew were found by patriots and got back to their base in Italy after 62 days.

* * *

BROUGHT home on rotational leave, the crew was entertained at the White House. Sgt. Martin was awarded the Purple Heart, Distinguished Flying Cross, Presidential Citation and Air Medal.

Following his leave at home, Sgt. Martin was assigned to Langley Field, giving final examinations to bombardiers. He was killed when the plane in which he was riding crashed on the takeoff.

Funeral services will be held at 9:30 a. m. Tuesday at the L. V. Barker Funeral Home, 12700 Hamilton, and at 10 a. m. at Visitation Church. He will be buried in Mt. Olivet Cemetery with full military honors, attended by a guard of honor from Romulus Airfield.

SGT. JOHN P. MARTIN
Hero killed in air c

In the Fall of 1944, Bob and Mariellen lived in Columbia, South Carolina, where he trained exclusively on the B-25 airplane. He was assigned to the 345th Bombardment Group and was part of the Air Apaches. She often spoke about those times as being happy and hopeful. She and Bob had little Punko (Julieann) and they enjoyed the time together. They often went on drives to see the beautiful fall colors, taking a picnic lunch and talking about the future. One thing they knew for sure was that the war made every minute with each other precious.

With Bob's deployment looming just ahead, Mariellen moved back to California with one-year-old Julieann, in December 1944. She and the baby took the train cross country. It was a long and lonely trip for her. She wrote to Bob--

The train, by nature of its routes, goes through the least attractive parts of the cities. The smokestacks and factories spew ugliness and sadness. I long for you to be with us, to cheer us with your humor and jokes.

Bob was finishing up his training in December in South Carolina. On the day of his brother Jack's fatal crash, Bob flew on a training mission where he had a deeply personal religious experience. He called Mariellen to tell her of his flight to the heavens. She replied in a letter--

It's wonderful in a way, isn't it, to see God's face. No matter how in a terrible storm - or in beauty so exquisite - that you can't speak. Bob, why didn't we kneel down to say our prayers at night? It seems funny that we didn't - it seems sacrilegious. We will, won't we, when you come home?

The news of his brother's death hit both Mariellen and Bob hard. After attending his brother Jack's funeral, Bob was on his way to Los Angeles to say goodbye to Mariellen. He had orders to report to Pearl Harbor for radar training and from there to the war in the Pacific. She had news for Bob. She was pregnant with their second child. Both were ecstatic. Neither of them knew then that Bob would miss the entire pregnancy and birth. They said their tearful goodbyes and hoped the war would end soon.

Chapter Five

1945

Bob Martin in front of his plane

"A fighter pilot is a combination of a mathematician and an athlete, a scientist, and a sharpshooter. He's got to know what goes on inside his plane. The heart of his fighter is steel and copper; its bloodstream is gas and oil. But its brain is the man who flies it."

***Wings for this Man* (A propaganda film produced in 1945 by the Army Air Force)**

The time allowed for pilot transition to combat planes varied throughout the war, but by May 1944, it was stabilized at ten weeks for bombardment transition. Fighter pilots received five weeks of training on obsolete combat types before being assigned to operational units, where they were given practice on current fighter types prior to tactical training. Transition to the specific aircraft to be flown in combat was the last stage of a pilot's individual training.

Upon completion of this stage, he was ready to start training as a member of an aircrew and a combat unit. Crew and unit indoctrination normally required about twelve weeks, after which the aerial teams were sent to staging areas to prepare for movement overseas.

My dad was awarded six pairs of wings during his training. He earned his flight engineer wings, bombardier and gunnery wings, navigator wings, pilot wings, and ultimately his senior pilot wings. His training took twenty-one months.

The 345th Bombardment Group my dad was assigned to was first activated at Columbia Army Air Base, South Carolina, in November of 1942. Flight crews trained there for five months before moving to Walterboro, S.C., for final preparation before deployment overseas. There were four squadrons that made up the 345th Air Apaches.

The 498th - The Falcons

The 499th - The Bats Outa' Hell

The 500th - The Rough Raiders

The 501st - The Black Panthers

Bob was proudly part of the 499th, *The Bats Outa' Hell.*

The 345th originally thought it was headed for Europe. Their maps covered that area, they were briefed by RAF officers, and it was assumed New York was the Port of Entry. The destination was secret, but as the first crew embarked on the long trip first touching down in Hawaii, then the Christmas Islands, Fiji, and New Caledonia, they realized they weren't going to Europe, and eventually ended up in New Guinea. A banner greeted them, which proclaimed,

"Through These Portals Pass The Best Damn Mosquito Bait In The World"

Bob wrote to Mariellen when he reached Pearl Harbor:

Be a good gal honey, & wait for me -
don't worry & don't get discouraged - please.
I love you - Oh I long for you so much.
I know now you are mine - & my love for
you is honest & true. 'Cause you are in my
thoughts always - I can't plan anything in
my dreams without you - - Even when I
think of Liz Taylor, I walk away with you in
my arms. I love you - two drinks tonight
no more - it's Saturday -
Are you working at the problem of one
extra bedroom - I've about decided we need
3 or 4 more kids - - all I want to do is
take you in between the sheets in my arms &
just live & love & love & love -
I better stop now -
no better news -
I love you
Forever
Bob

74

In February 1945, Bob flew from Pearl Harbor to New Guinea. He was stationed at Port Moresby. As part of the Air Apache 345th Bombardment Group, he joined the Fifth Air Force there. He was trained in and assigned to fly the Mitchell B-25 and the B-26 Marauder.

The majority of B-25s in American service were used in the war against Japan. The aircraft's potential as a ground-attack aircraft emerged during the Pacific war. The conversion from the B-25 level bomber to the "strafer" role began in August 1943, and one the Air Apaches would become famous for.

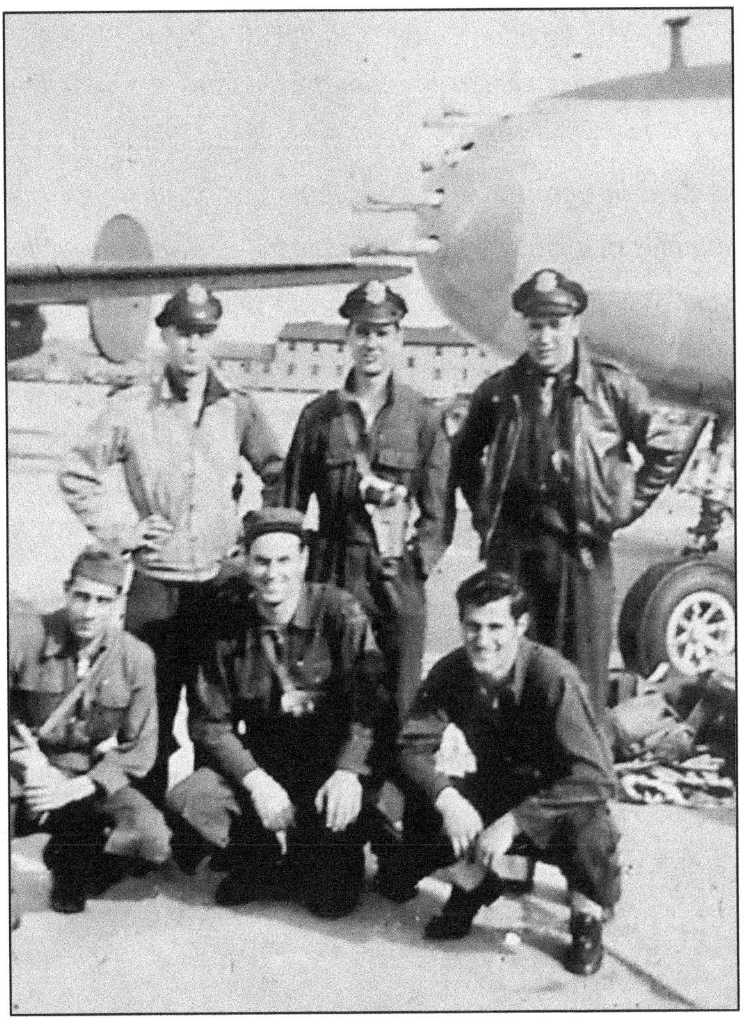

Bob (top right) with his crew in front of their plane

March 1945
Los Angeles

Bob Darling,

This is supposed to be last night's letter. We went out to dinner last night and when we got back Paula was here. She stayed until about eleven o'clock, so I had to go to bed. I didn't have time to even say very good prayers.

Oh honey, the last month has been a hectic one. If my letters aren't as cheerful or trusting as they should be - don't ever think it's your fault. I'll catch myself all of a sudden at the end of a week or so and it will seem like I've made a little hole and climbed into it to shut everything out. So then out I climb and try again. It's the things that matter that make you feel and sometimes the feeling is a hurt one instead of a happy one. You are what matters to me and sometimes I guess not having you makes me feel so much that I can't do it anymore. Only I can, so there it is. I love you!

What kind of a Sunday are you having? By the time you get this, you'll probably have forgotten. Maybe you're out dozing in some warm sunny place getting a tan that will make people turn around three times instead of only twice like they usually do. And we'll hear someone whisper - "Who is that movie actor?"

Darling, I love you my husband. Let's not be getting chummy with any brown girls on any islands with one tree. Oh Bobby, take care of yourself! Bobby darling, just be careful and bring yourself back to us in one big, fat piece. I love you,

Forever,
Mariellen

My father showed us this book he brought back from the Pacific. It was issued by the military soon after he arrived in New Guinea. He wrote this note to me when he was going through his things before he passed away.

"After spending 3 days in the jungle they give you this book in case you go down in the interior. It's funny reading now."

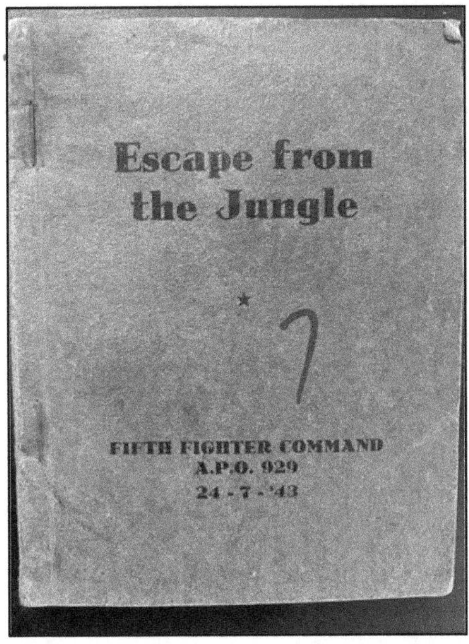

Table of Contents (Continued)

March 1945
New Guinea

Dear Beautiful,

It's raining this afternoon - the typical thunderous, terrible, and treacherous thunderstorm.

Starts off with a sunshine and roses kind of day. Then the breeze dies. Clouds seem to form from nowhere. Soon the world is dark grey. It's a dirty color and a dirty feeling. The very quiet of the land seems to have stopped the world on its daily rotation. The entire universe seems stilled and waiting - then on the distant skies comes a small black dot; growing as it comes toward you - until you can see the whirling mass of wind and rain and clouds almost as a gaping mouth ready and eager for prey.

Still, you only feel the presence of power - feel it not with your senses but with your heart - the leaves move not a bit, tall grass and bushes don't move or bend with a breeze.

It's all dead around you - yet you somehow know that in the very air is power, potent enough to tear the very earth from its core. And then it comes. With the first damp breeze you hear and see the thunderous bolt of lightning, seemingly sent from the heavens to mark the beginning of a show of might and power.

The rain and wind and lighting that follow are watched in breathless interest. They seem so mighty - so powerful you wonder why you are not struck down - why you are allowed to live through it - yet, God stays his hand and soon tiring or rather feeling He has made you aware of His might long enough - He removes it.

As suddenly as it comes, it is gone. And even now as the gutters carry the water away I can look up and see the blue sky and white clouds - I don't have the slightest idea where it goes but it sure disappears.

I can feel the sunshine now - it's warmth and love and your smile that is sunshine to my soul. I know after every storm the sun will come back and encourage and strengthen us little guys who are not as blessed by God as you are.

Gotta go take a shower and shave for tonight. I work all nights this week.

Wish you were here to dress up for. Seems as if I never did enough for you. Thank God you are mine and I pray each day I may be worthy of you -

P.S. Hey, I forgot to say I love you - when August 14th rolls around and it's a boy - we'll name him John Patrick Martin and call him Jack and if it's twins and we get a gal we'll name her Kathleen Theresa Martin and call her Terry. And later on, in 6 or 7 years - we'll have one more - a little gal - and we'll call her Mariellen and nickname her Jill.

Forever I adore you, my beautiful wife,

Bob

April 1945
Los Angeles

My Darling,

Bobby honey – Hi. I hope you're all dry and comfortable now. Does the sun ever shine there so you can hang stuff up? You're really up a creek (river) if you can't.

There were four letters waiting for me today. One dated the 12th, one the 13th, one the 14th and another the 14th. If you knew how they -- but Bob, you do know how much they mean. Honey, ask me for whatever you want. That's a pleasure you can give me - sending you things. I had a box all packed to send to you, but it weighed two pounds too much, so I have to repack it. Darn. It doesn't cost much to send a box. Even if it did, it would be worth it. How would you like to have a box full of boards? For your floor!

Just a note, darling. It's such a nice time of day. Dinner is nearly ready, and the smell is floating through the house of hamburgers and mashed potatoes. It's evening - long golden shafts of light float in through the west windows, Julieann is fed, and all of the hardest work is done. I love you - at times like this more than ever.

Julieann cried for about an hour tonight before she went to sleep. She's been getting some bad habits, so I let her cry. That's hard. She finally quit when she was playing with the shade I had pulled down at the door and it flew up on her. She was so startled and surprised that she couldn't cry. Bob, I can just see you laughing at her. She started to cry again, but she just couldn't. She kept looking at the shade and being surprised all over again.

Honey, I called Father Bowling this afternoon. He's coming to see me Friday. Just like that. At least he's going to try. I washed my hair today and Punkie's. I made hers into long curls - mmm! I cut out some rompers for our baby today, Bob. Now I'll sew them up and the baby will have something to arrive in.

Honey, I'm so thrilled about this baby, what will he look like - will he have black curly hair, blue eyes, long legs and a twinkle in his eye like his daddy? Darling I love you. I love you with all my heart. Through all this dark night between us - my love must reach you - in each whisper of wind - in each moonbeam that shines on you - in each bit of beauty that may touch you whether it's one you have to dream of, or a real one that is there where you are. I love you. Goodnight Darling.

Forever yours,
Mariellen

April 1945
New Guinea

My Dearest Wife,

My darling, I love you - I adore you - here's a kiss, X, just for you. I hate mail - it's horrible and evil - These guys expect you to be interested in their letters & to listen while they read stupid parts of very commonplace letters like they were masterpieces of literature. They show their pictures around like no one else has a camera or knows how to use 'em.

They sorta smile when you don't get any mail & offer to buy you a beer - so they can force you to listen to theirs.

But mostly the reason I hate to go to mail call is the hope and then the disappointment - the physical hate you feel for the mail boys who you know have lost or deliberately misplaced your letter.

And then in the evening hours - the dreams that have to be mended because of the unconscious resentment you've built up from lack of a letter - only the proud and the wealthy can afford resentment and you're very humbled here, but the feeling passes thru, swiftly.

But this entire gauntlet has me feeling worse than all the others - the feeling of loneliness - of being left out. That's the worst. Now I understand and began to feel the hurt you felt when I, by being a real fool, gave you no indication of my love - you poor little gal - I never knew how much it hurt. I didn't help myself anyhow, for I never gave my love to anyone - just kept it stubbornly locked up - 'til now.

So now you can see how and why mail has become a sort of bugaboo - but our love and our dreams - are great enough to carry me through.

Please don't take this too seriously. I'm trying to sorta make a joke - oh my darling don't even think of leaving - your heart won't let you - it's too close to mine, they are tied together and nobody can bust them apart. Please believe that. Write and tell me you'll be waiting and loving me.

I suppose it doesn't make good sense reading this - I'm not sure I wouldn't laugh too. But this is the way my heart seems to say it - in the evenings the words tumble out not the same as the words inside. I need your hand to guide me. I need you.Someday I'll write you a letter, let it stand overnight - rewrite it - edit it - justify the lines - correct the spelling. It'll be perfect, just like the dreams are.

I'll do one tonight - get it started that is. Only now it seems important to get the words out. In the fear of losing you, the thoughts and words get tangled and all I can dream of is the terror of you going away - terror for me. Please write - please - writing it seems so inadequate. Damn anyhow -I love you.

Bob

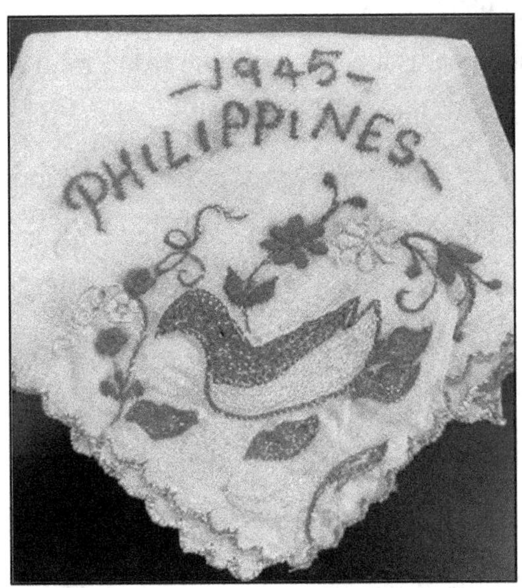

Handkerchief from the Philippines

April 22, 1945
Los Angeles

Bob Dearest,

Hello Honey - another Sunday. I love you more every Sunday that comes. Thank gosh tomorrow is Monday again - mail! Hah! I wait behind the door for the Postman to come and I peek out the window - and the second he has left the mail I pounce on it. About half the time though, he rings the doorbell. That's always good because it means a letter from you with "postage due." Just to receive a letter from you is heaven, honey. I love you,

Forever yours,
Mariellen

For members of the armed forces, the importance of mail during World War II was second only to food. The emotional power of letters was heightened by the fear of loss and the need for staying in touch during the tough times of separation. The impending danger and uncertainty of war made letter writing even more important. Emotions and feelings usually expressed only on special occasions were written to ensure devotion and support. Back on the home front, mail from loved ones overseas was a reassurance of love and health.

In an article written for the Army and Navy Journal (December 1943), Postmaster General Frank C. Walker detailed the efforts the government took in "marrying the expertise of the Post Office Department with the U.S. Army and Navy." At the time he wrote the article, Walker said the department had 1,300 U.S. Post Offices serving Army posts and camps in the United States. Another 400 Army Post Offices functioned in more than 50 foreign countries. Additionally, the U.S. Navy had postal facilities on ships and on-shore stations in 2,000 locations.

Here is more from the article, headlined "The Postal Service at War," quoted directly:

"An example may make clear just where it is that the Post Office Department withdraws from the picture and the military authorities assume control. Mrs. Richard Roe, in Chicago, knows that her son is overseas, but is not sure just where he is stationed. She addresses her letter as follows: 'Private William D. Roe, 3200000; Company F, 167th Infantry, APO 810, c/o Postmaster, New York, N.Y.,' and drops it in a mailbox. At the Chicago post office, it is canceled, sorted, and tied in a package of letters labeled 'New York, N.Y. – Military Mail.'

Still under the Post Office Department's immediate control, it arrives at the New York Post Office's Postal Concentration center, a great building whose entire facilities and hundreds of workers are engaged exclusively in the final processing of the mail before it is handed over to the military authorities.

The package goes through sorting processes for separations according to the branch of the service, such as Infantry or Field Artillery, and secondly, according to the

Company or similar designation. Finally, Mrs. Roe's letter is placed in a package of mail for members of Company F, 167th Infantry. The package then goes in a mailbag to the New York Port of Embarkation Army Post Office. It is here that the Army assumes control.

The Army knows where Company F is located; we do not. Private Roe's letter goes by ship or plane to the overseas A.P.O. through which Company F gets its mail.

The package is handed to the mail orderly of Company F, and he delivers the letter to Bill Roe.

If Bill has been transferred, or if he is in a hospital, the Army Directory Service furnishes the new address and the letter is re-dispatched, or re-sorted, for delivery at the new location. When letters are misdirected, long delays occur. Ship sinkings have meant the loss of many thousands of letters. Mrs. Roe's letter to Bill is one of approximately five billion which go to and from the armed forces in a year."

The fact that both my mom and dad saved all their letters for all this time serves to prove how important they were. My parents said they read, then re-read, and read again these letters. They looked for innuendos tucked into phrases and paragraphs. They both tried to stay upbeat, yet their frustration over not being together clearly comes through in their writing. According to the dates and content of their letters, my parents lived together only 144 days of their first four years together. That is just thirteen percent of their time. The other eighty seven percent of their communication was done through the mail. Separated by distance and by uncertainty, their letters were a lifeline extended during crucial times.

While the exact origins of the phrase "Dear John" letters are unknown, it is commonly believed to have been coined by Americans during World War II. Large numbers of American troops were stationed overseas for months or years, and as time passed, many of their wives or girlfriends decided to begin a relationship with a new man rather than to wait.

To the deployed "John" receiving such a letter made time stand still, yet the earth still rotates. Everyone knows someone who got a "Dear John" letter. Such a letter could have a profound effect on a soldier. Once received, it would often shatter a man as there was rarely anything he could do, being thousands of miles from home.

The Smithsonian Institution has opened an exhibit on letter writing during WWll at the National Postal Museum. On display are letters collected from soldiers serving time abroad as well as their families back home.

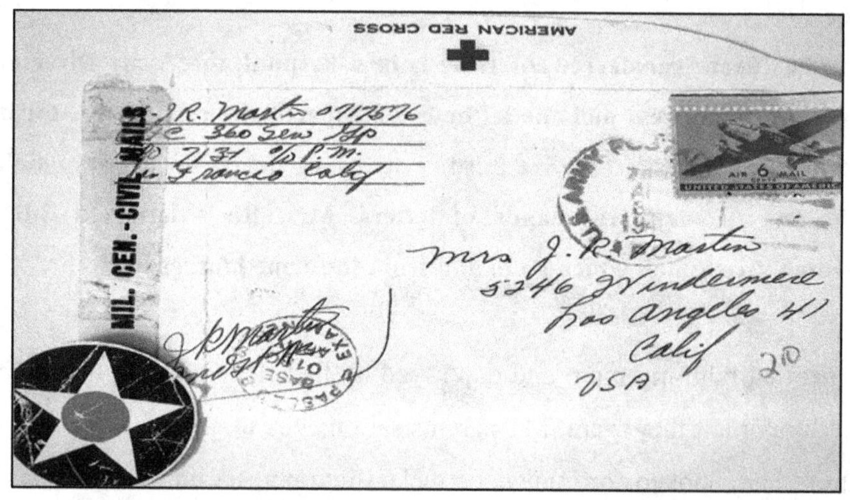

On April 4th, 1945, the first Nazi concentration camp, Ohrdruf, was liberated by the 4th Armored Division and the 89th Infantry Division. It was the first Nazi concentration camp liberated by the U.S. Army. When the soldiers of the 4th Armored Division entered the camp, they discovered piles of bodies, some covered with lime, and others partially incinerated on pyres. The ghastly nature of their discovery led General Dwight D. Eisenhower to visit Camp on April 12, with Generals Patton and Bradley. After his visit, Eisenhower cabled General George C. Marshall, the Head of the Joint Chiefs of Staff in Washington, describing his trip to Ohrdruf:

"... the most interesting— although horrible— sight that I encountered during the trip was a visit to a German internment camp near Gotha. While I was touring the camp, I encountered three men who had been inmates and by one ruse or another had

made their escape. I interviewed them through an interpreter. The visual evidence and the verbal testimony of starvation, cruelty, and bestiality were so overpowering as to leave me a bit sick. In one room, where they had piled up twenty or thirty naked men, killed by starvation, George Patton would not even enter. He said that he would get sick if he did so. I made the visit deliberately, in order to be in a position to give first-hand evidence of these things if ever, in the future, there develops a tendency to charge these allegations merely to 'propaganda.'"

US soldiers view the bodies of prisoners in Ohrdruf

While it felt like the war could be winding down, there was little cause for celebration. This, perhaps, was one of the first realizations as to what had happened in Hitler's Germany.

April 1945
New Guinea

Dear Beautiful,

How's the world over there where it's still yesterday and as a matter of fact evening - just about time for you to put Punkie to bed.

I'll bet she is precious now, and very lovely and oh so sweet and huggable. Just like a little puppy.

How's Jackie coming along with his mommy - is he behaving and growing according to doctor's orders? And you take care of yourself - keep beautiful and don't get all tired out. I want you well - plenty of sleep, and at least four weeks in the hospital. You have to be fully recovered by the time I return and ready to go places 'cause I have lots of plans.

Just learned of Roosevelt's death. A great blow. The greatness of that man will not be appreciated or known for years to come. The greatest Commander of forces the nation has ever known - Democracy is at its crossing point today. His passing is the greatest loss to the people of the world that they have suffered in the last hundred years. The men over here feel very deeply about his passing. They were not behind all of his political beliefs, but they were 100% behind his ideals and actions as Commander in Chief of the Army.

I remember how stunned we all were to hear the loud speaker announce that the Commander in Chief is dead.

The flag is to fly at half-mast - a fitting tribute - for one month of mourning.

It's raining here now. It's pouring and the floor of the Red Cross hut here is two inches in water, and the roof is leaking like a sieve.

The water blows in here, and flows in and flows out, like a river. Three hours from now, the floor will once again be dry and hard. Funny land. I've got to close now. Got plenty to do - we are moving out shortly, and I will write when I can tell you our new APO and stuff.

Baby, I miss you more than you ever know - and will know cause I won't tell you - only know this. I love you above all else and worship your very picture. Honey, we are going to be the happiest two people in all the world.

I love you,

Bob

In April of 1945 Franklin Delano Roosevelt had been president of the United States for a record 12 years. Often referred to by his initials FDR, he was an American political leader who served as the 32nd President of the United States. Famous for his quote, "the only thing we have to fear is fear itself" he passed away on April 12, 1945. President Roosevelt served through most of the Great Depression. He implemented his "New Deal" domestic agenda in response to the worst economic crisis in U.S. history. His third and fourth terms were dominated by World War II. FDR is often rated by scholars as one of the three greatest U.S. presidents, along with George Washington and Abraham Lincoln.

Bob wrote to Mariellen about how the president's passing affected the troops in the Pacific. An interesting glimpse into how news from Stateside was received.

By the time my father was sent to the Pacific Theatre, it was widely known to be an assignment that would likely not turn out well. The U.S. casualty rate in the Pacific was three-and-a-half times of that in Europe. The lives of 103,000 Americans were sacrificed to defeat Japan, along with more than 30,000 Britons, Indians, Australians, and other Commonwealth servicemen, many of whom perished in captivity.

Soldiers, sailors, and airmen never felt entirely healthy during Asian or Pacific service. For those fighting the land campaigns, disease and privation threatened the men's welfare. Malaria and dysentery were widespread and deadly. The Army educated their servicemen about the importance of using netting and taking their anti-malaria medication, but many felt the medication wasn't necessary and often didn't take it on a regular basis.

"Hello, suckers," Tokyo Rose taunted from Radio Japan.

Tokyo Rose was the name given by Allied troops in the South Pacific during World War II to all female English-speaking radio broadcasters of Japanese propaganda. The programs were broadcast in the South Pacific and North America to demoralize Allied forces abroad and their families at home by emphasizing the troops' wartime difficulties and military losses. Several female broadcasters operated under different aliases and in different cities throughout the Empire, including Tokyo, Manila, and Shanghai. The name "Tokyo Rose" was never actually used by any Japanese broadcaster, but it first appeared in U.S. newspapers in the context of these radio programs in 1943.

American cartoons, films, and propaganda videos between 1945 and 1960 tend to portray her as highly sexualized, manipulative, and deadly to American interests in the South Pacific, particularly by leaking intelligence of American losses in radio broadcasts.

The Japanese were a difficult enemy to fight. Major-General Douglas Gracey wrote;

"The capture of a Japanese position is not ended until the last Jap in it (generally several feet underground) is killed. Even in the most desperate circumstances, 99 percent of them prefer death or suicide to capture. The fight is more total than in Europe. The Jap can be compared to the most fanatical Nazi youth and must be dealt with accordingly. Extreme methods would have to be used to defeat them."

In July 1944, American troops in Saipan, the largest island of the Northern Mariana Islands, witnessed a "banzai" charge, where nearly 4,000 Japanese soldiers charged American troops and fought to their death. They were following the last orders of their commander, Lieutenant General Yoshisugu Saito, who had called for this all-out surprise attack to honor the Emperor before committing ritual suicide.

American troops also witnessed a different atrocity as they saw women grabbing children and jumping from cliffs rather than submitting to capture in the final days of the Battle of Saipan.

In the summer of 1944, Masaichi Kikuchi graduated from a Japanese Army Officer school. He went home to his tiny village north of Tokyo, bursting with pride and keen to show off his new uniform. In a community where everyone lived in thatched cottages with their plough horses, chickens, and silkworms, he was a celebrity.

"We grew up in a world where everyone who was not Japanese was perceived as an enemy," he said. "Chinese, British, American. We were schooled to regard them all as evil, devilish, animalistic."

To be captured by the Japanese meant almost certain death. The brutality was raw and savage. Along with living in horrific conditions, the majority of POWs worked as slave laborers to keep Japan's heavy industry going.

They toiled relentlessly on docks, airfields, in coal mines, shipbuilding yards, and in steel and copper works. Random beatings, torture, and solitary confinement were dealt out at will by sadistic, brutal, and unpredictable captors. The average prisoner received less than a cup of dirty rice a day. The amount was so meager that gross malnutrition could lead to a loss of vision or unrelenting nerve pain.

My father carried with him two "Blood Chits." In the simplest terms, a blood chit is a message, written in local languages, that a lost service member can present to most anyone who might help. It offers a rough description of the predicament– "I am not from here and would like to get back to where I belong" –along with both a request for aid and the promise of a reward for assistance.

Many U.S. flight crews that flew over Asia had their "blood chit" sewn to the back of their flight jackets. Some units added the blood chit to the crew's flight suits. Before aircrews departed, each crew member is issued a chit, and each associated serial number is recorded. This way, if the service member later is missing and someone contacts the United States and says that they have found him or her, the serial number provides a means to verify the claim's legitimacy.

The amount awarded for authenticated claims ranged from $50 to $250, depending on the theater. The chits were carried by many crews, particularly fixed-wing aircrews, and by other service members deemed to be at what the military calls a "high risk of isolation." The U.S. military continued to use blood chits during the Korean and Vietnam wars.

Blood chit usage is now classified. History has shown that once any of our enemies discovered the successful return of an American with the assistance of local person(s), it often resulted in the torture and death of the helpers. In some cases, the death of their entire family and even an entire village resulted in this information becoming known.

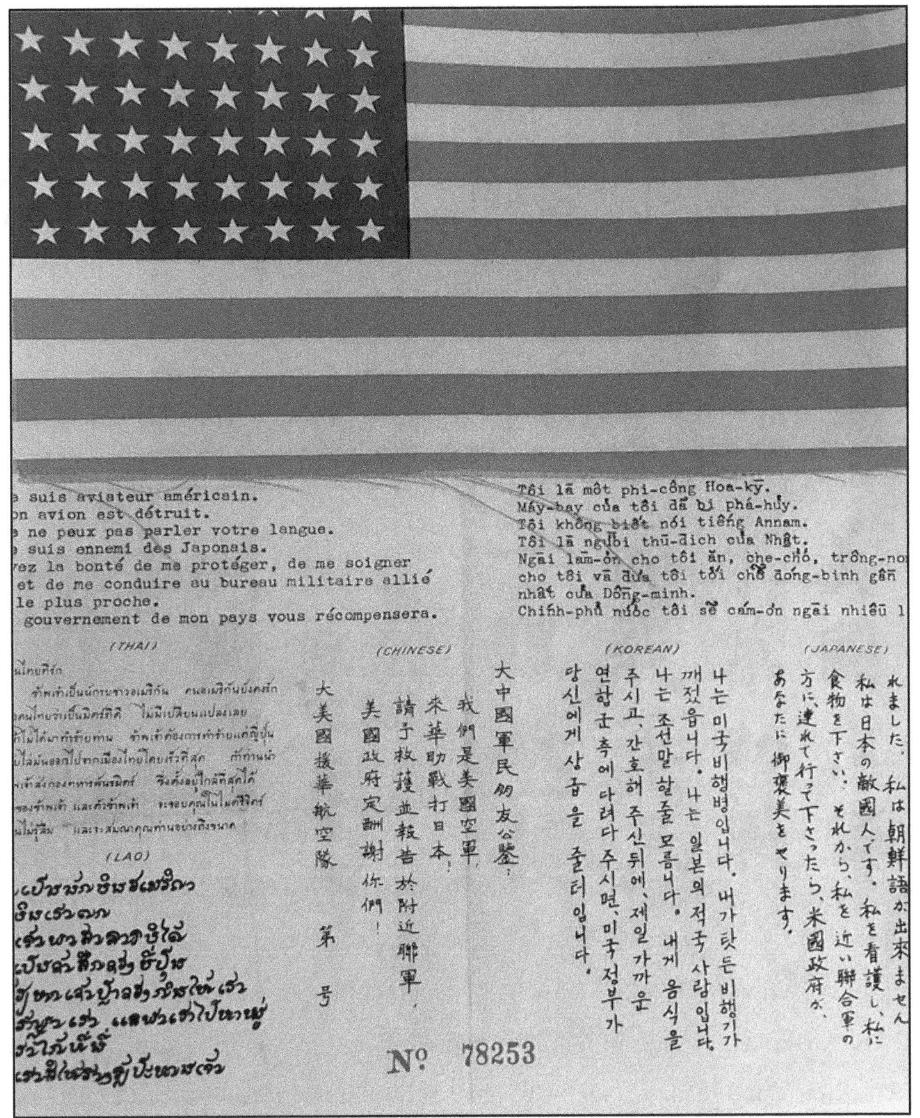

This Blood Chit my father carried is made of silk, and measures 8 ⅛" x 12". The flag is red, white and blue. Written in French, Vietnamese, Thai, Lao, Chinese, Korean, and Japanese and topped by an American flag, the message describes the flyer's predicament. "I am an American Aviator. My plane is destroyed. I do not speak your language. I am an enemy of the Japanese. Have the kindness to protect me, to care for me and to take me to the nearest allied military office. My government will pay you."

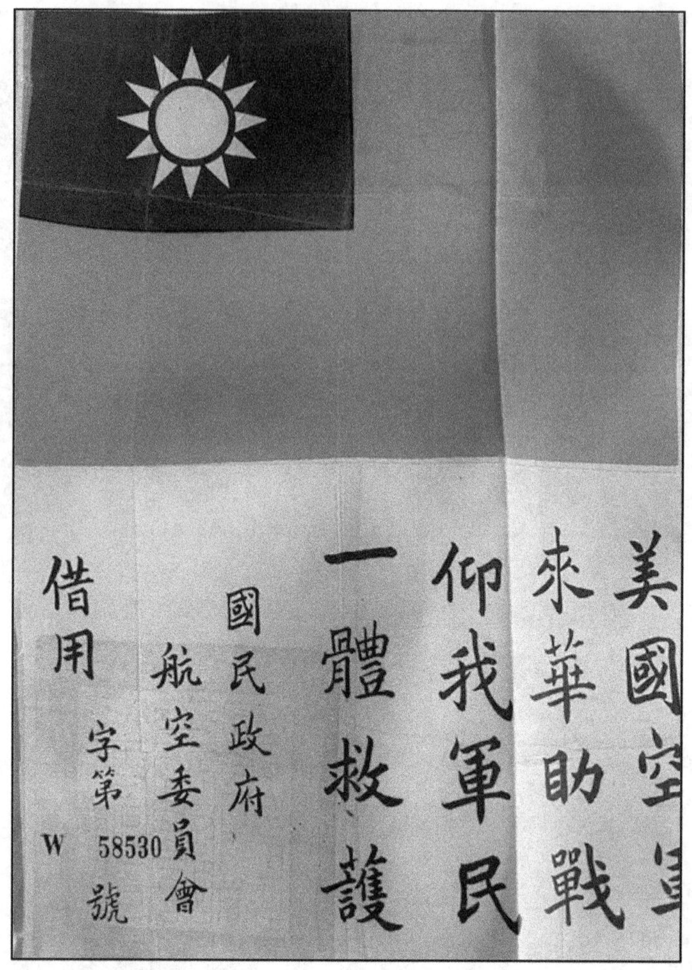

The China-Burma-India (CBI) Blood Chits had the flag of Nationalist China at the top (in red and blue) with a message in Chinese below. These officially-issued Blood Chits were 7½" x 9½" inches and made of silk. They had serial numbers and were stamped in red with the chop (seal) of the Nationalist Government's Commission for Aeronautical Affairs, or Air Force Committee. The stamp was carved out of ivory. There were two printings of these official CBI Blood Chits. This one, given to members of the Flying Tigers, shows a Chinese Flag. The serial number was originally intended for use in identifying the pilot. The "W" to the left of the serial number stands for Washington. The second version also added characters indicating "American" in the second column (from right). Translation of this version: ***"This foreign person American has come to China to help in the war effort. Soldiers and civilians, one and all, should rescue, protect, and provide him with medical care."***

May 1945
Los Angeles

Dearest Bob,

Here it is - night again. We "ate out" tonight. There is a place up here on Huntington Drive, nearly to Monrovia, where they have hamburgers with a couple of slices of tomatoes, onions and pickles for 35 cents. It cost $1.85 for all of us, including milk and coffee. It's a nice place too. The Plantation it's called.

Did I tell you I ran out of gas yesterday? Well?? I did. On the way to the bank. I had to walk about eight blocks. I washed my hair this morning. The vitamins are doing their stuff. I wasn't half as tired as I have been. I love you.

I got the swellest letter from you about five minutes ago. Oh darling, I hope you come home soon. It's hard to realize a world without war, isn't it? Especially where you are and that is all there is. But I am beginning to get a ray of what it will be like. There are so many things I want to talk to you about and it seems like they'll be better in person. Then we can talk when we are together. You do all the talking. I'll just listen and watch you. All my life won't be long enough to watch you in - darling. I love you. With all my heart and soul, I love you. Goodnight my dearest precious.

Forever yours, Mariellen

Mariellen and Julieann

May 1945
New Guinea

Dear Beautiful,

It's a wonderful morning for sleeping - it's raining now and has been for several hours. It's wonderful to sleep with the rain

pit-patting on the tent roof.

I read a couple of mystery books lately. I usually don't like them. I grew away several years ago when I had read a number. Again, I am fascinated by the mystery and the murderers name - but most always I find a reason to quarrel with the plot of the story and there are many questions as yet unanswered in my mind when it's all over. But for want of anything better and for escape I will read them with my tongue in cheek and enjoy them.

The rain has let up considerably now and it's humid as heck. It's now about 10 o'clock. I got up around 8 and played a few games of chess with Bill Mason and then drank a can of tomato juice I'd been saving. Then repacked - a bit - all of my luggage. I'm a packrat and I've got to rearrange it every so often.

Now for a letter to you and then to chow, and then perhaps we will go North this afternoon. These planes fly out of here all the time regardless of weather or anything.

I bought a mattress cover at quartermaster yesterday and now in lieu of a mattress I use it as a sheet. Sure feels nice. I've been smoking my pipe and using the chess men Cloyd sent. They are really nice.

I'm going to take a sunbath this afternoon if I can, so I'll have a real deep tan. Enjoy life while you can. Here we can't eat, drink and make merry - because - the food is barely meant for ingesting - the drink is chlorinated water and there are no Mary's to make. But we sunbathe and sleep when it's not raining, or we aren't busy. Honey - I love you - you are so much with me these days. So deep in my heart and my soul.

Forever Yours,

Bob

All through the Spring of 1945, the 345th Bombardment Group took part in sweeps of the seas around Hong Kong, helping damage Japanese merchant ships. They also attacked a convoy off the Indo-China coast and sank two warships and a 956-ton merchant ship.

In addition to close ground support missions on Luzon, my dad's group worked their way over Formosa (Taiwan). On April 4th, twelve aircraft from the group attacked Mako harbor, sinking or damaging six merchant ships. On April 6th, a Japanese destroyer and two warships were sunk, the destroyer having earlier shot down one aircraft from the 345th during a sweep over Yulin. Formosa was the target again on April 15th when the group attacked railroad yards, bridges, and factories in Nanseiho and Osono airfields in the north of the island.

When my dad arrived home after the war, he brought back photographs (marked restricted) with him, taken from his plane. These were highly prized possessions in our family, and as kids, we often "shared" them at school. Though we couldn't get my father to say much about his experience, these pictures, and the fact he kept them, told a story all their own.

He wrote on a separate piece of paper - ***"Here's a couple of photos I managed to escape with.***

Picture #1 – low altitude (25 to 50 feet) bombing. You had to have a couple of parachutes in order to slow down the descent, so you could get out there before the blast. High resolution photos – You can take a glass and see a lot of detail. The copilot's window is shot out – the guns in the upper turret are turned right – ground fire I suppose at the plane. This was taken by the lead plane. Although the bomb bay doors were open, no bombs had yet been dropped."

Picture #2 – Two long seconds later they crashed. This was one of the many small refinery and factory areas in the lower islands."

The Air Apache's "claim to fame" came when, virtually unaided, they carried out the aerial blockade of the China Sea.

The war in the Pacific was a battle of distance, and it was a long way from their base at San Marcelino in the Philippines to the shores of China. Unloading the B-25's of all unnecessary weight increased their range. The four forward-firing package guns were removed, along with the two flexible waist guns. The crew of six was reduced to five by the elimination of the armorer-gunner. The tail guns were then manned by the radio operator, who crawled back to the turret as the target was sighted.

As ship after ship left the Japanese ports, the Air Apaches swooped out of the skies and sent the ships to the bottom of the sea.

Newspapers across America ran pictures and articles on the front pages. Headlines, such as *"The Mast Height Marvels Do It Again"* or *"Here Are the Secrets of The Apache Success,"* made them famous. While this success was not without cost, it did lift the morale of the group. The 345th made tactical history.

B-25's of the 345th Bombardment Group Sink Frigate Near Amoy, 6 April 1945

(From my dad's collection)

The 345th Air Apaches moved from San Marcelino to Clark Field, the U.S. Military Air Base in the Philippines, on May 12th, 1945. At San Marcelino, the Air Force constantly battled the wet conditions that made roads and landing strips muddy and messy.

Clark Field was far better than San Marcelino. The tents had screens, and most had tin roofs. There was running water and even benches in the mess hall.

The last days at San Marcelino had seen the end of Japanese shipping off the China and Indo-China coasts. Efforts were now directed toward knocking out all military installations on Formosa (Taiwan). The Air Apaches also gave ground support in Northern Luzon, where they routed the enemy in heavily-defended positions in the Cagayan Valley and Belete Pass areas.

Toward the end of June with Formosa no longer an important military target, and the campaigns of Luzon and Okinawa in their final stages, the Air Apaches suspended combat operations and began a training program in preparation for new targets on the Japanese homeland.

It was during these last flights that my dad came down with pneumonia. His lungs may have been weakened by a previous case of pneumonia during training two years earlier. The doctors told him his flying days might be over. For the time being at least, he was grounded. He was devastated.

June 1945
New Guinea

Dear Beautiful,

It's just ten o'clock here now and the evening seems so long and drawn out. The evening shift is kinda slow. The reports are interesting, and the messages keep you on your toes. We get the radio and telephone news from the States first, so it's not really too bad, I guess.

The nights have been hot. The weather this season resembles New Guinea. Rain, damp air, high humid conditions and no breeze. This is the weather they use when they wish to describe the jungle as "steaming".

Tomorrow or Tuesday I have to meet the final flying board and they are going to decide what I will do. As I told you, their job is pretty well cut and dried - "ship 'em home" - no one has been kept here yet. I'm going to try just the same.

Funny me telling you this by letter - when I know you don't even know I'm at 5th Bombardment Command yet and won't for a couple of days at least. By the time you get this letter my fate will have been already decided by many days.

But even though you are far away by letter - you are always close by in my dreams.

Ever in my heart.

Forever I love you,

Bob

July 4th, 1945

Los Angeles

Hello, My Beloved,

Today was the Fourth of July. It didn't seem like a different day. There will probably be some fireworks tonight. I haven't gone out to see.

You know those papers that you said had articles written in them about your Squadron? Pop is going to get them tomorrow. I can hardly wait to see them.

Bob, the Presidential Citation is really something - did your group get it for all the missions and dangerous stuff or for one particular mission?

Oh darling, I love you. My big honey - hey when are you coming home? Let's be giving some details. How much suspense do you think I can stand? For gracious sakes - I'm afraid you'll walk in any minute - and I'm more afraid you won't. You're going to have my blood pressure up to a hundred and umpity.

There wasn't any mail delivered today, so I'll have to wait impatiently until tomorrow to hear or see if there is any mail. Anyway, I love you, Darling. I'd give so much to have you come home soon. Golly, Bob, I love you. Goodnight my husband - I love you,

Forever Yours,

Mariellen

The war in Europe had been over for weeks now, however the war against Japan was heating up. Mariellen hoped Bob might come home since he'd been grounded because of his lungs. But that hope was not shared by Bob.

My father did not want to come home. He wanted to continue to fly and fight with his group. I can imagine the desire to return home to his family was strong, yet he felt compelled to finish the job he started with the Air Force. He wanted to get back in the air.

10 July 1945

Morning Beautiful,

It's almost noon now. I really have been up since 0700 and have been working, but now I'm free until 1300 - so I will let my hand have free rein over that which my heart loves most.

I've no orders yet. They are effective the third, but will not be cut until tomorrow, but as it is now it's just a job in headquarters communication.

I guess they thought I knew so much about the radio compass that I would be a good communications officer. Or it's just a job until my final papers are settled or something.

I'm kinda discouraged - the job is an important part of the army and probably communications is the most security conscious part of the Air Forces. But frankly, I don't know what I'm doing here. I believe it is just temporary duty - my orders say "detached service from 345th group" (or will say it), but I'm assuming it's not anything but a job until they get ready to send me home.

Nevertheless, it's a job and I shall do my best in it. I don't quite know what's what yet however.

It's nice here. I'm hoping I can fit in and do a good job for as long as I am here.

Not much more to tell darling. I'm sorta discouraged, yet I know I'm honest and with you at my side the future looks bright as hell. I can see only hard work, love, happiness and success ahead for us.

I want you always at my side. I'll always want you there no matter what happens.

This is the time that will test my courage and my will power and I'll make the best use of my time and my work. I've no doubt that I will be assigned from here to the U.S. and home - It's not what I wanted.

But we will accept it and make the best of it. We can even use it to an advantage. You know you can use most anything if you just face it and call a spade when you see one.

I think together we are bigger than anything in the world - and you know something, we may have to prove it.

Anyhow I love you - I guess I love you more today than yesterday - well I know it.

I've been hearing all about transportation difficulties - I hope Mother can make it out.

Not much more from here. Will write again this evening. My address is - Headquarters 5th Bomber Command APO 710 -

Anyhow, whatever comes - it's a break to be here for a little while - shows they think I'm some good.

Forever,

Love, Bob

In July 1945, Mariellen was 8 ½ months pregnant with their second child and on her own in Los Angeles.

July 26th, 1945
Los Angeles, Calif.

Hi Sweetie,

Hey, I love you darling. We went over to pay the hospital this morning, where the baby will be born. Bob it is the loveliest place. It is just like a huge estate with beautiful grounds. Trees, trellises, ferns - you can't even see the Sanitarium from the street.

Churchill was defeated. I'm glad. I think he is past his usefulness. Only it seems sad to see him go.

Let's not be worrying about your little wife. Darling, I am going to recline on my pillows in the hospital for two whole weeks if I can stand it. They say you feel marvelous around the tenth day and feel ready to take on the whole world. Besides I'll be lonesome for my Punko. They won't let little kids in the hospital.

How is the world treating you tonight, Lt. Martin? If the weather keeps on like it has been, Eagle Rock is going to turn into a damp and steaming jungle.

I love you Robbie. I'll be so glad to see you tall and slim and wonderful again. And eager. Oh honey, honey, come home soon. I love you,

Forever yours,
Mariellen

*** In her next letter, Mariellen tells Bob what she told his mother about his pneumonia and not being able to fly for a bit. My mom later told me he didn't want to tell his parents he'd been quite sick and in the infirmary for two weeks. They'd lost his brother in a military plane crash less than a year before, and he didn't want to add to their stress.**

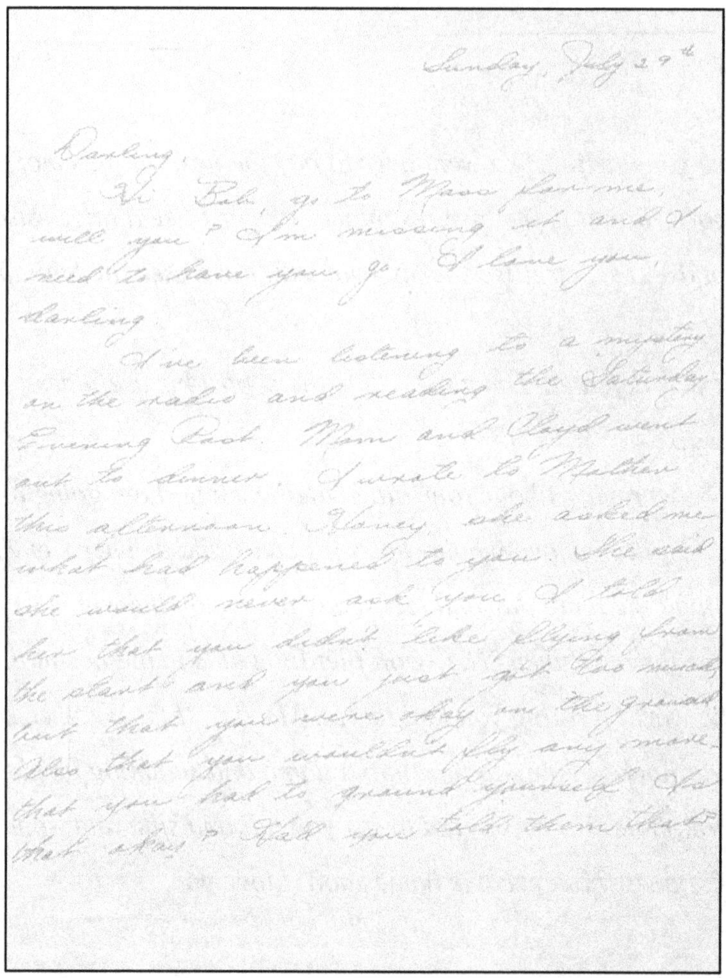
Sunday, July 29th

Darling,
Hi Bob, go to Mass for me, will you? I'm missing it and I need to have you go. I love you, darling.
I've been listening to a mystery on the radio and reading the Saturday Evening Post. Mom and Lloyd went out to dinner. I wrote to Mother this afternoon. Honey, she asked me what had happened to you. She said she would never ask you. I told her that you didn't like flying from the start and you just got too much, but that you were okay on the ground. Also that you wouldn't fly any more. That you had to ground yourself. Is that okay? Had you told them that

Continued...

What do you think of this picture of a dining room? Bobbie, this is sort of the feeling I want my house to have (our home - okay?) Sunny and lovely and cool all thru it. Do you like it? If we have any money saved when you start back to school darling - I think we'll get along swell. I like to take care of a budget - figure out where the money has to go. I like order and a place for even the small things. I like to fix things and shine and polish - maybe it's the beauty that shows when things are at their best.

I can be planning about you darling - do you know that every thought of putting on a shirt and slacks or my prettiest dress has a whisper of "how would it look to Bob" in it. Julieann is asleep - it's nearing 9:30. What are you doing, darling, I wonder? Poor little Punk. She has bruises all over her. She fell off the chair and banged her arm. Someone asked where we got her a permanent the other day. Her hair curls and waves all over. And her eyes are big, and exactly the same blue color as yours. It doesn't seem like it's nearly time for Jackie to be born. Time is all screwed up. Jeepers, another week almost by without a breath to stop it! It's still hot here but not quite as hot as it was. And Wednesday, it will be August darling. It amazes me to see the time fly by, yet it also seems so long.

Here it is - that night again - will you take my arm, sir? And shall we go waltzing or to the Opera? By the way honey, you know of your last letters that were opened by the censors, only one had anything cut out. And then about two words. None of your letters have been censored since you were moved. Your letters are like talking to you, Bobbie. Only I wish I could really talk to you, Darling, I miss you so awfully.

No mail from you for four days. Every time there is space, I begin to think things, asking" maybe" questions.

Bob, I love you. I wonder if you're coming home. There are so many things I want to talk to you about and it seems like they'll be better to wait.

Bob, nothing seems very interesting. Everything seems kind of suspended waiting to know which way things are going for you. Coming or staying darling? Darling I love you. Lt. Martin, you are the man of my dreams. And what dreams! May God take care of you until there won't have to be dreams, Bob darling. Forever and ever,

Yours,

Mariellen

Mariellen received no letters from Bob for over two weeks. The letter that eventually reached her was written in a new and different format. Rather than a daily letter, he wrote one letter that included snippets from July 23rd to August 14th, over three weeks' time.

Sections had been censored, redacted and cut out, probably because he wrote about the Atom bomb.

Bats 'Outa Hell Patch

July 23, 1945
Okinawa

Beautiful,

Hey don't scold me honey. I'll tell you all about my desire and hope to stay in after I come home. It's our business - Hey, I love you.

July 26. Thanks for the 15 bucks. I'm cashing it in the U.S.A. though. They won't cash m/o here on Okinawa. We use Yens and you need a truck to get paid. You get lots of rest even now. Thanks for the dough.

July 27. We won't finish the dishes at all. Just throw them away. I've done my dishes over here. A mess kit 3 times per day. We are going to say our prayers together every night and thank God (I am) that you are my wife.

July 29. I don't like the blue dining room. Missing Mass eh? You understand me so well. You must be straight from Heaven. I adore you - and it's our home not your home. I am more than a boarder, see! I hereby order you to get some of "Thorne Smith's" stuff to read. Then you'll see partly the philosophy of the "post-war mad Martins". I love you

You are my beautiful baby wife. God, I love you. I could never look at another gal with you on my mind - and you are never off.

August 1. New month - Hey I love you.

August 7. How about putting on a sweater to greet me when I arrive. The Atomic Bomb is terrible - depressing - but like gunpowder can be useful if correctly used. Sometimes I'm too

conservative I think - best I just keep still - I miss you so much - like the world is a clock and when you're away, someone forgot to wind it and it just stopped - no good.

August 8. You will have to can every fall and spring for several years honey - so be stocking up on supplies. Nothing as precious as my children 'cept my wife.

August 9. I love you, I adore you my beautiful.

"P.S - I dreamed we had the loveliest little Girl "unquote. You double dealing traitor.

August 14. Take a good long rest honey. Now I mean I need one more letter. The last one was dated the 22nd and that's all I've gotten. The rest will reach me soon.

I love you

Bob

Later, though evasive, my dad explained the unusual format he used in writing this last letter. He had no time, nor routine. He'd been reinstated as a pilot (after being grounded with pneumonia). His unit had temporarily suspended combat operations and was in a training program on Okinawa in preparation for new targets on the Japanese homeland.

Several new bombing techniques were developed, new crews were checked out, and in general, the squadron was made ready for the war across Japan. This program required top security measures as they prepared for a move to Ie Shima, an island off the coast of Okinawa, both of which had been recently seized from the Japanese. From Ie Shima, the Air Apaches travel-ranged to Southern Japan and Korea. For the first time, the group would be able to bring the war to Japan's Home Islands. The field at Ie Shima was primitive.

It was one big field of mud with weeds everywhere. The men noted the mud was of a peculiar quality and was at the same time as slippery as grease and as sticky as warm tar.

At the start of August 1945, the 345th Bomb Group was bigger than it had ever been. The unit needed to be ready. The invasion of the Japanese Home Islands was planned for November and was expected to be a bloodbath. Many of the men who had been there for a year or longer were sent home. My father wanted to stay. The new crews coming in had not seen combat, and my father had. Now he would be one of the senior officers, having been in the Pacific for six months.

Some authorities estimated that the invasion of Japan would cost up to half a million American lives or more. The Japanese would lose many millions more, both military and civilian.

In these final months of the war, the Allies prepared for a costly invasion of the Japanese mainland. The war in Europe had concluded when Germany surrendered on May 8th, 1945, and the military turned their full attention to the Pacific Theater.

The Allies called for the unconditional surrender of the Imperial Japanese armed forces in the Potsdam Declaration on July 26th, 1945, the alternative being "prompt and utter destruction." Japan ignored the ultimatum, and the war continued.

My dad brought back these propaganda notes.

He explained them as follows in a letter: "**This is a type of message the Japanese dropped to the South Pacific natives, telling them how great the Japanese Nation was and how they were winning. (But written in Japanese).**" Leaflets were printed in red, blue and white.

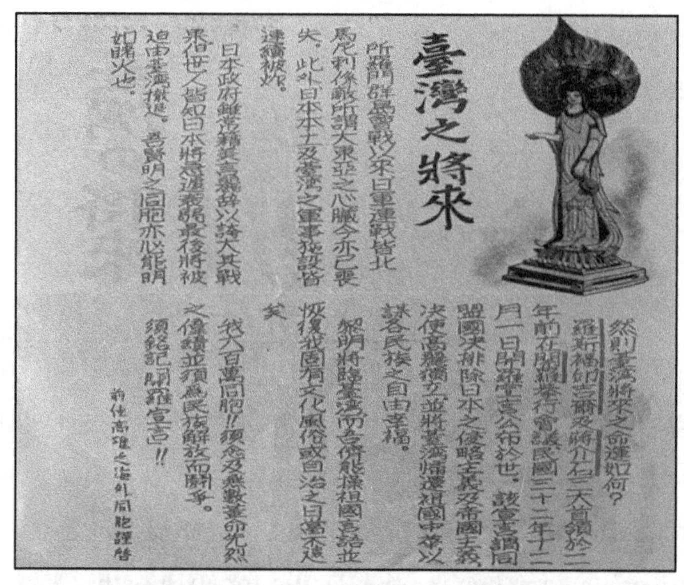

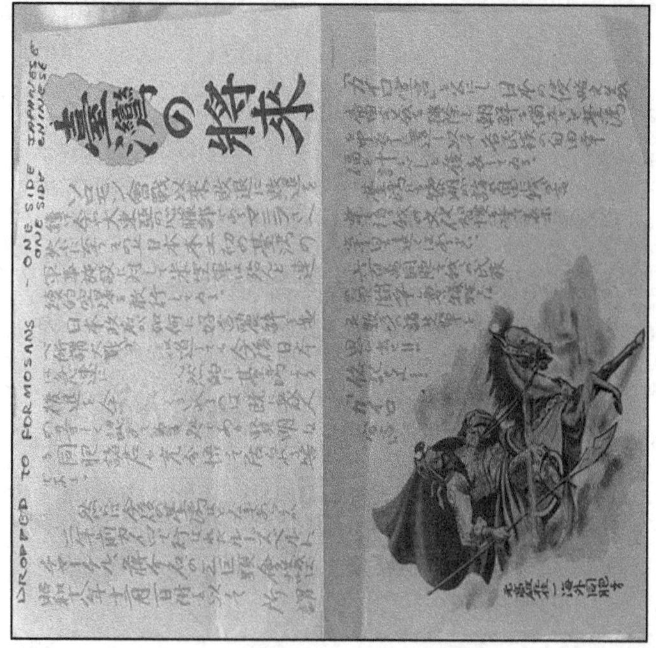

My dad also brought back propaganda leaflets that the U.S. dropped over Japan.

"A sample of the leaflets we (the U.S.) dropped over the Japanese as we came closer to the main island. It is supposed to show that America was winning and about to invade. But luckily for us, we didn't have to work our way through the country."

"Read from right to left"

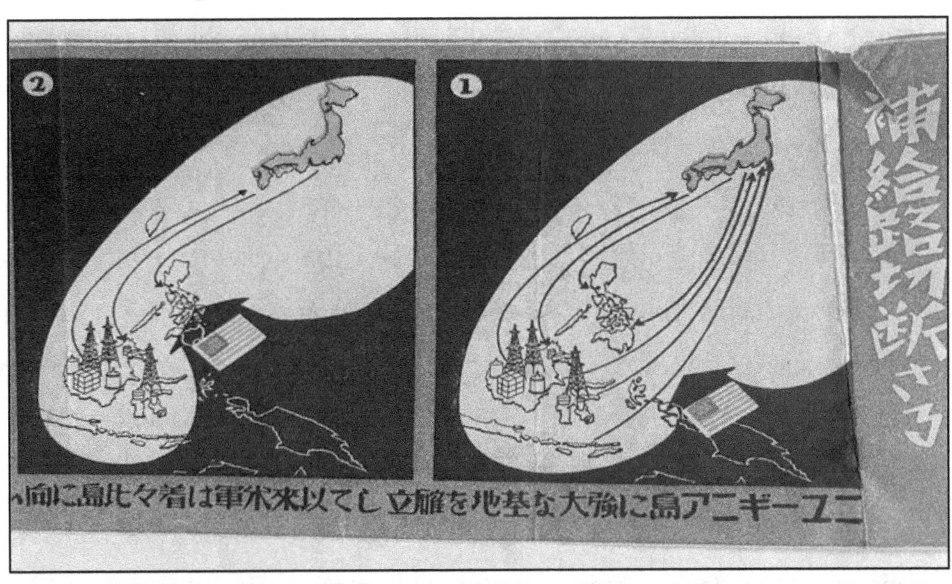

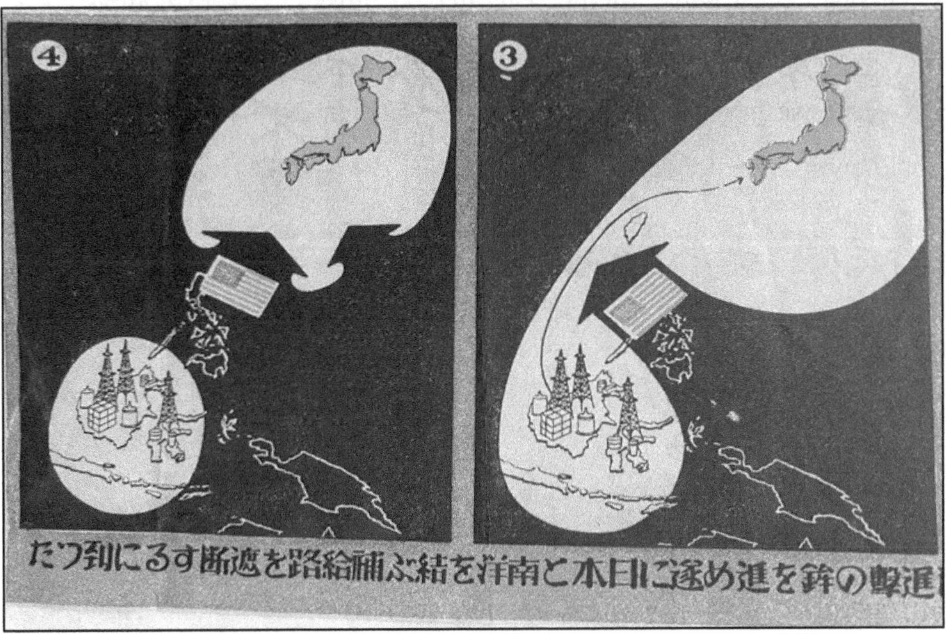

The first raid on the home islands of Japan began by hitting targets on Kyushu, on July 29th, 1945. The 345th Air Apaches concentrated on enemy radio and radar installations, factories, and shipping off Korea, Kyushu, in the Sea of Japan and the Inland Sea. The intensive training program paid off with dividends in the enemy's home waters.

In August, the feeling of imminent victory was in the air. The Soviet Union's entry into the war, followed shortly by the Atomic Bomb, proved the final blows. Even these did not stop the nightly red alerts, the searchlights scanning the skies, and the flashes of bombs and Kamikazes hitting ships in the harbor.

The first Atomic Bomb was dropped on August 6th, 1945, by an American B-29 bomber, over the Japanese city of Hiroshima. The explosion wiped out 90 percent of the city and immediately killed 80,000 people; tens of thousands more would later die of radiation exposure. Three days later, a second B-29 dropped another A-bomb on Nagasaki on the island of Kyushu in Japan, killing an estimated 40,000 people.

But the Japanese didn't give up. Not yet.

During the first fifteen days of August, though negotiations were underway and there remained little doubt of the outcome, 11 missions were completed. Combat operations continued at an accelerated rate, and what seemed to be a premature idea of early peace was soon forgotten. The result was that 29,600 tons of enemy shipping was sunk, but the cost to the U.S. was high. The Air Apaches lost 12 planes

August 7, Tuesday 1945
Los Angeles

Bob, I love you,

I've no mail from you for five days. Bobbie, what does it mean? It could mean you have been sent to the hospital and then will be home. It could mean - oh darling - but it probably means that the mail has been held up. Sweetheart, I love you so very much. I'll dream tonight of your arms around me and my head against yours because that's what I want so terribly. The loneliness of being without you and the touch of your hands and voice makes a shadow that won't ever be here again when you get home. Maybe for tonight a dream will help.

Goodnight Bobbie Darling

I'm still home. Golly Bobbie, I've been off the beam lately, but now things seem a lot better. Even if I haven't heard from you.

When you get home, I'll tell you all the things I've wondered that you might be doing. No mail from you for nearly two weeks.

Remember my telling you about Peggy? And how long Ralph was supposed to be gone? Well he arrived. She wrote that he got here on the 7th of June, but he was in terrible shape. They were going to do brain surgery but then didn't have to. He's on a 90 day leave now and will probably get a medical discharge. Darling we are lucky people. Peggy says she is terribly happy. At least Ralph is home and now he can get well.

I've been getting more stuff done the last couple of days. My sweaters are all clean and they look swell. Punko's room is cleaned and ours too. It seems like I've been just fooling around and then there was a lot to do.

Bob, that atom bomb is really something. That's all we've heard the last day. I wonder if heating, lighting and power will be changed in the next couple of years. And what will it do to all phases of industry. One professor said that the industrial revolution wasn't even a start of what this will be. I'm even wondering if you are having something to do with this.

Forever I love you,

Mariellen

The Air Apaches mission on August 15th, 1945 was halfway in the air when word came that offensive operations had ceased. In a radio address, Japan's Emperor Hirohito announced his country's unconditional surrender citing the devastating power of "a new and most cruel bomb."

Back in Los Angeles, word of the surrender arrived a day earlier, on August 14th. That was the day that Mariellen gave birth to their second daughter. A little girl named Theresa Kathryn Martin. My parents had discussed what they would name her if she were a girl but didn't get to communicate during that time. They later said they almost named her Victoria Jane for VJ day.

August 20, 1945
Los Angeles

Darling,

Terry was born on V-J day - the 14th of August - Tuesday here. She started to be born about a week before, only she got a little way - then stopped.

We were eating dinner in the kitchen and I had a spoonful of food about halfway to my mouth when my water broke. I was so surprised I just sat there with the spoon in the air, and in a pond of water. Away we went to the hospital and she was born in about three hours at 10:14 p.m.

Bobbie it does hurt so. It hurts so much that if they don't give you anything (a hypo) pretty quick, you don't get anything. But it wasn't long and now it's past. But darling, I cried - not from hurting, but I needed you so. Anyway, Terry is just like Julieann - everyone thinks so. I think she looks more like you - her face is shaped like yours. She is going to be blonder than Punko and have curly hair and long, long eyelashes. And Bob, I feel fine this time. Golly, I thought I was okay last time.

Honey, I can't even dig up any remorse for no boy. Little Terry is just as dear as Punko and two baby girls together will be precious. We still have lots of time for a Jackie and a Bob. And I still want them as much as ever. I think the more you have the more you want. I miss you so. Darn it my Bobbie. Hey, do you ever have exciting dreams? Bob, do you? I dreamed this morning that I got three letters from you today. But I didn't.

I love you, Bob, and I think you're wonderful.

Yours, Mariellen

After Japan's surrender on August 15th, 1945, there was little to do but wait for the surrender to be formalized. The U.S. sent a set of instructions to Japan ordering the emperor to send military and government representatives to Ie Shima, from where they would be flown to headquarters in Manila. There they would sign the documents that would officially end the war.

The instructions read, in part,

"The party will travel in a Japanese airplane to an airdrome on the island of Ie Shima, from which point they will be transported to Manila, Philippine Islands, in a United States airplane. They will be returned to Japan in the same manner. The party will employ an unarmed airplane ... such an airplane will be painted all white and will bear upon the side of its fuselage and the top and bottom of each wing green crosses easily recognizable at 500 yards. The airplane will be capable of in-flight voice communications, in English, on a frequency of 6,970 kilocycles."

The Japanese prepared two Mitsubishi G4M "Betty Bombers" as instructed. The armament was removed, both were painted white with green crosses on their wings, fuselages, and tails.

Japanese Surrender delegation and the Betty Bomber in Ie Shima

The 8th Fighter Group flying P-38's and B-25s of the Air Apaches were selected to escort the aircraft carrying the Japanese representatives to Ie Shima.

On August 19th, 1945, six B-25s from the 345th Air Apaches searched three areas in pairs for the planeloads of Japanese that had left Kyushu in the early morning. They were given the great honor of intercepting and escorting the two Japanese "Betty Bombers" that were transporting the peace emissaries who were to initiate the Japanese surrender.

My dad had the privilege and honor to be chosen as part of this group.

As they landed in Ie Shima, long lines of men lined the runway. It seemed everyone on the island was there. The Japanese were mostly generals and diplomats. They boarded another plane, MacArthur's C-54, which took them to Manila. A more formal ceremony - intended for a broader audience - would take place on September 2nd, 1945, aboard the USS Missouri.

By the end of August, over four hundred men from the 345th Air Apaches were sent stateside. By the middle of September, over five hundred more departed for home. Bob was not among them.

My dad mailed home this newspaper dated September 5th, 1945. It was called the ***Fifth Air Force Invader*** *and* was published on the base in Ie Shima. He wrote at the top - **`All the news we get -`**

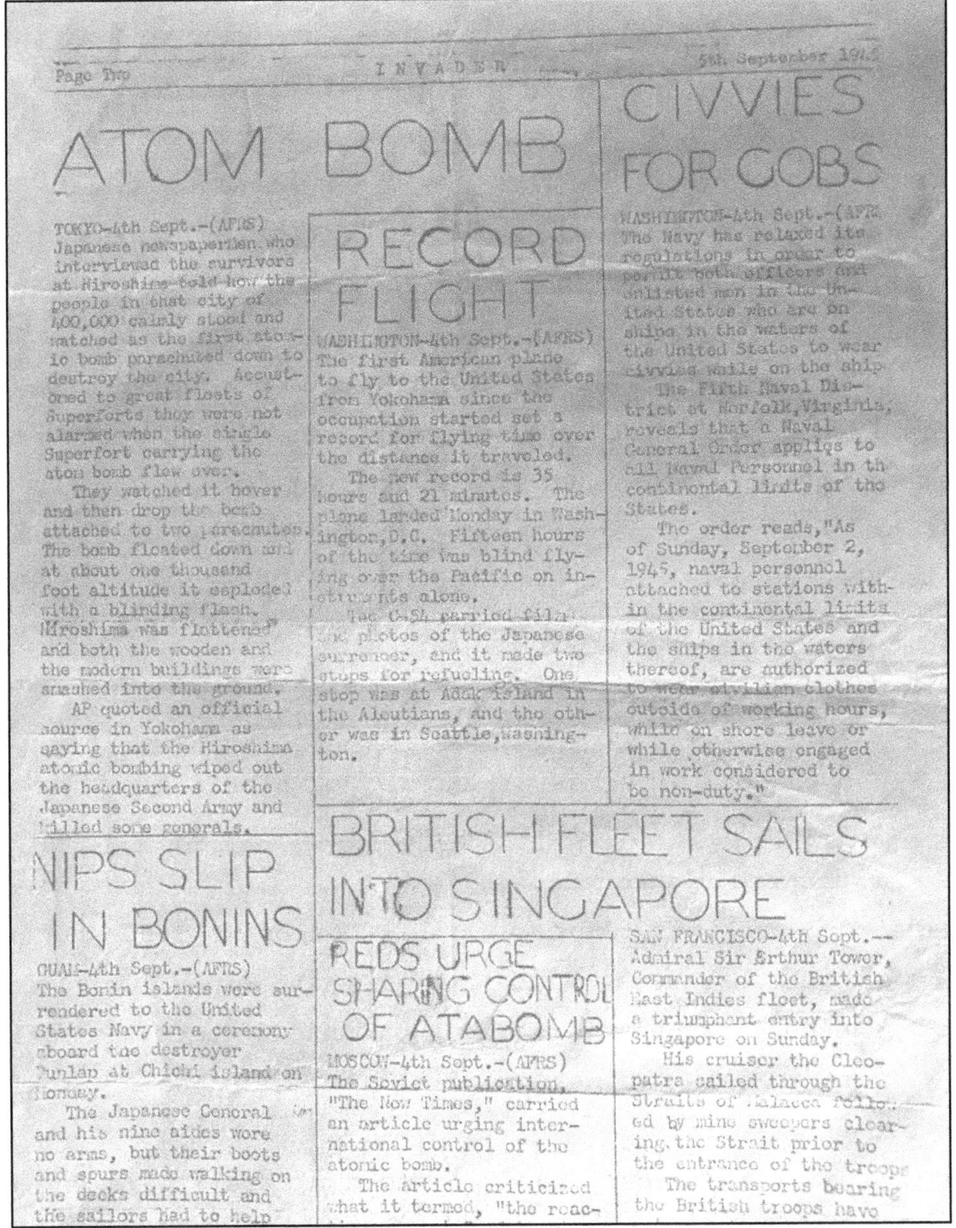

Page Two INVADER 5th September 1945

ATOM BOMB

TOKYO-4th Sept.-(AFRS) Japanese newspapermen who interviewed the survivors at Hiroshima told how the people in that city of 400,000 calmly stood and watched as the first atomic bomb parachuted down to destroy the city. Accustomed to great fleets of Superforts they were not alarmed when the single Superfort carrying the atom bomb flew over.

They watched it hover and then drop the bomb attached to two parachutes. The bomb floated down and at about one thousand foot altitude it exploded with a blinding flash. Hiroshima was flattened and both the wooden and the modern buildings were smashed into the ground.

AP quoted an official source in Yokohama as saying that the Hiroshima atomic bombing wiped out the headquarters of the Japanese Second Army and killed some generals.

RECORD FLIGHT

WASHINGTON-4th Sept.-(AFRS) The first American plane to fly to the United States from Yokohama since the occupation started set a record for flying time over the distance it traveled.

The new record is 35 hours and 21 minutes. The plane landed Monday in Washington, D.C. Fifteen hours of the time was blind flying over the Pacific on instruments alone.

The C-54 carried film and photos of the Japanese surrender, and it made two stops for refueling. One stop was at Adak Island in the Aleutians, and the other was in Seattle, Washington.

CIVVIES FOR GOBS

WASHINGTON-4th Sept.-(AFRS) The Navy has relaxed its regulations in order to permit both officers and enlisted men in the United States who are on ships in the waters of the United States to wear civvies while on the ship.

The Fifth Naval District at Norfolk, Virginia, reveals that a Naval General Order applies to all Naval Personnel in the continental limits of the States.

The order reads, "As of Sunday, September 2, 1945, naval personnel attached to stations within the continental limits of the United States and the ships in the waters thereof, are authorized to wear civilian clothes outside of working hours, while on shore leave or while otherwise engaged in work considered to be non-duty."

NIPS SLIP IN BONINS

GUAM-4th Sept.-(AFRS) The Bonin islands were surrendered to the United States Navy in a ceremony aboard the destroyer Dunlap at Chichi island on Monday.

The Japanese General and his nine aides wore no arms, but their boots and spurs made walking on the decks difficult and the sailors had to help

BRITISH FLEET SAILS INTO SINGAPORE

SAN FRANCISCO-4th Sept.-- Admiral Sir Arthur Tower, Commander of the British East Indies fleet, made a triumphant entry into Singapore on Sunday.

His cruiser the Cleopatra sailed through the Straits of Malacca followed by mine sweepers clearing the Strait prior to the entrance of the troops.

The transports bearing the British troops have

REDS URGE SHARING CONTROL OF ATABOMB

MOSCOW-4th Sept.-(AFRS) The Soviet publication, "The New Times," carried an article urging international control of the atomic bomb.

The article criticized what it termed, "the reac-

Tuesday, Wednesday, Thursday
Okinawa September 1945

My Dearest Beautiful,

I love you my wife - Wish you were here with me tonight - To love you is all that I want out of life.

Tuesday - Nothing unusual except a lot of work. The Air Force has sure left us a mess - we are headquarters now. Food terrible - I love you - worked until two thirty typing and doing a few odds and ends. I love you.

Wednesday - Larry got me up at 8:30 to go down to Yonton with him. I had expressed the desire to go a couple of days before - so - half awake with my toothbrush in my pocket and my shoes untied, we grabbed x jeep and were off.

I had some misgivings about going but when we had finished our work there we stopped into the 380 for lunch. They had fresh meat. It was sure tasty.

It was sorta unfair, the way we just got into line and ate with the rest of them.

Then over to quartermaster and we got a pair of shoes with the boot strap tops. It has been cool at night lately and Japan is a three blanket place.

The road back was rough - we left Yonton at 3:00 and at 3:15 the typhoon struck. Rain, both hot and cold - from all directions and like a waterfall in amount of force.

We were so cold and wet and discouraged and damn...one raincoat between us.

The road was slippery, and, in most places, it is one-way anyhow and darn narrow at that. So it is only logical that certain parties would try and get through and slide off.

There were many hold-ups like that - too many - we were very wet when we arrived here. Our jeep was new - fairly - and had no holes drilled in the floor yet to allow the water to run out - so we were flooded inside as well as outside.

But after a nice hot cheese sandwich - only it wasn't hot and there was no bread - only cheese, we dried off and went to bed - disgusted - by knowing I would dream of you - Out of the cold into a warm blonde -

Thursday - The food is terrible. I know it's not right to bitch but darn - They have had nothing but canned crap for a month now.

Breakfast today - two pancakes - canned and heated. A spoonful of syrup (shortgut), a bit of cooked bran and a cup of canned milk for the cereal. Nobody drinks the coffee anymore - anyhow they are short of it most of the time - and that's all.

Lunch - Spam (or canned meat), cabbage or spinach (canned) and maybe some fruit or maybe not. That's all (water).

Dinner - Tea - or sometimes coffee, Spam, canned potatoes, beans and every other day, some crackers or (1) one piece of bread. No butter or jam. That's all.

It's no good. The fellows wouldn't complain in New Guinea or while the war was on - but now there is no excuse for it. Some outfits are eating - but mostly on the island, everything is bad. We have considered seeing the general - some of the fellows are writing to congressman (silly), but darn you are hungry all the time - 'til finally you try to fill up on a smile and then you find out you can't get seconds - crap.

Well it rained all day today. I slept until 10:00 and then worked all afternoon on some crap.

The evening was spent in dreaming of you.

Our tent leaks - so I covered my stuff and came down here. The rain has beat down and blown away the bugs so it's nice to write in the evenings. Hey, I love you - I adore you my sweet darling. I miss your arms about me - My nights are spent in dreaming of you - only you - I can't seem to remember how beautiful you look -

My baby darling. The only reason for me is you - life isn't, you are. I only wish I could tell you of the many ways and things I want from you - the many things I want to give you.

I love you,
My Beautiful,
My Wife

Bob in New Guinea

Bob's plan was to stay in the military. If he voluntarily delayed his departure home, he would "make rank," which meant he would move up a rank to Lieutenant and therefore be entitled to a higher pay grade upon arriving back in the States.

Plans for the group to be sent home as a complete unit, along with the rest of the 5th Air Force, were derailed by two typhoons. A typhoon in early October all but leveled what was left of the camp area in Okinawa and made rations and housing a serious problem.

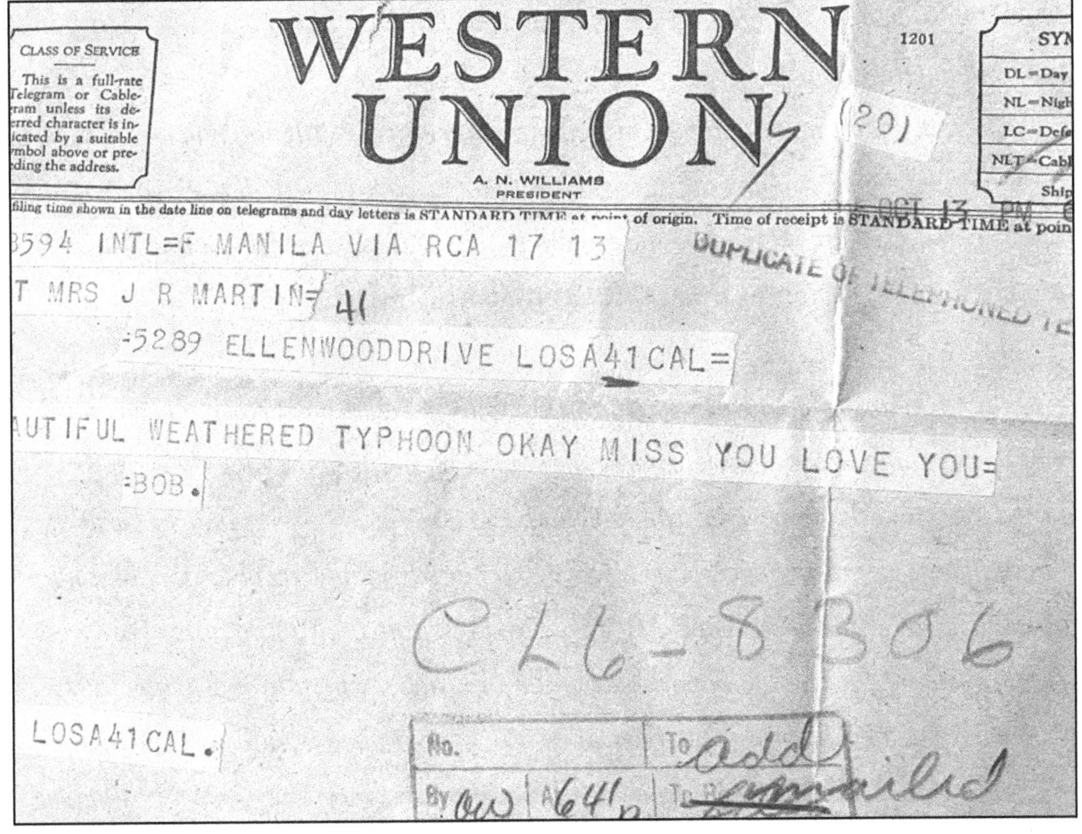
CLASS OF SERVICE
This is a full-rate Telegram or Cablegram unless its deferred character is indicated by a suitable symbol above or preceding the address.

WESTERN UNION

A. N. WILLIAMS
PRESIDENT

1201 (20)

DL=Day
NL=Nigh
LC=Defe
NLT=Cabl
Ship

filing time shown in the date line on telegrams and day letters is STANDARD TIME at point of origin. Time of receipt is STANDARD TIME at poin

OCT 13 PM

DUPLICATE OF TELEPHONED TE

3594 INTL=F MANILA VIA RCA 17 13

T MRS J R MARTIN= 41

=5289 ELLENWOODDRIVE LOSA41CAL=

UTIFUL WEATHERED TYPHOON OKAY MISS YOU LOVE YOU=

=BOB.

CL6-8806

LOSA41CAL.

No. | To add
By ow | A641 | To mailed

October 1945
Los Angeles

Darling,

I see where I'm doomed to a life of rubbing backs. You and your daughters, Lt. Martin are just alike. Terry can cry long and hard but let me turn her on her tummy and rub her back - and everything's fine.

Where were you when you sent me the cable? I was pretty worried darling. I'm so glad you're okay. It sounds trite - only how could I give it more expression? But you know I'm so helpless - I could pray for you - and I did all day long and for days, until you sent me the cable.

Darn it, I built myself up for your coming home just a little too much I guess. You don't mind if I give you just a little of this do you? I could weep all over your blouse front my beloved. In a day or so the rightness of it will make sense - it does already, but it's weeping for the loneliness inside my heart. I love you.

Tuesday

Bob, I'm disgusted as all something. Oh golly honey, I'm sure up a creek until you come home. This being dependent on people no matter how nice they are, is about the worst thing there is. You have to be so careful about this and so careful about that - you must control your temper and not stir up any trouble. You arrange your day to fit whatever anyone else wants to do. What you want to do or how you feel is beside the point. Oh honey, they couldn't crack a whip any more effectively over your head in the army than here even if they do it unconsciously. They just haven't had to adjust to anybody, it's still their house, everything goes on as before - and you adjust to their convenience. What a life.

Afternoon -

Since I had a nap I can see the bright side of things again. Hey darling, I love you very, very much.

Forever, Mariellen

October '45
Okinawa

Here 'tis honey,

We are all done here - from now on, no more jobs - just here - and every day a letter. I'll bitch, but not too much - there will be no chance of coming home for several months -

My records are scattered from here to Korea and back, and I've got to get 'em all fixed. Besides. being occupational troops makes it longer. Mac says all men with 85 points from here are home or on their way by now. Some shit - if I had a dollar for every man in this theatre who has over 85 points, I could buy my way home.

I love you a lot tonight darling - more than I could have dreamed I would ever love anyone. I've found myself and now I don't want to leave you ever. I love you beautiful. Golly, I miss you. Send me some pictures - a copy of you and punkin in the backyard at Columbia.

I haven't as yet received any packages - don't, yes do - send 'em anyhow. I have word from postal authorities that two of them were in this theatre - but are now gone - destroyed - tough!

Hey, I love you,

Kiss the gang for me
Your loving husband

I adore you beautiful,
Forever, Bob

Sunday, October '45
Los Angeles

Hi Big Honey,

How's my sweetheart tonight? I love you.

Oh boy, oh boy, oh boy, did I get the work done today. Now tomorrow morning the only job I have to do is fold about umpity clothes, so I'm going to get a lot of put-off letters written.

Folding the clothes is the only job besides feeding Julieann and Terry, sterilizing bottles, making formula, bathing Julieann and Terry, changing Terry a dozen times, giving Julieann drinks, taking her to the bathroom, giving Terry water etc. etc. That's just routine you know. Toss it off as an everyday thing. It's only a big day when it's like today - doing a big washing, going to Confession, Mass and Communion and ironing all afternoon. I feel so good. I still could have gone dancing tonight with you and had a wonderful time.

I just stabbed a bug with my fountain pen.

Terry's having her ten o'clock bottle and she's really smacking her lips over it.

Well Bobbie darling, it's time for me to catch my ten winks. Please come home. Oh precious, what I'd give to be in your arms tonight and sleep. Nothing could be so dear as that. Knowing you were here and close - golly it would be pure Heaven.

I love you my Lt. Martin -

Yours,
Mariellen

When Japan officially surrendered on September 2nd, 1945, the demand for rapid demobilization from soldiers, their families, and Congress became unstoppable. A total of 85 points were needed for eligibility to return stateside. The point system, called the Advanced Service Rating Score, had the objective of achieving equity in demobilization. Soldiers were given one point for each month of military service and one additional point was given for each month of overseas service. Each battle star or decoration earned a soldier 5 points. Soldiers who had earned that number of points were to be demobilized as soon as transport back to the United States was available. The points required for demobilization were reduced several times, reaching 50 points on December 19th, 1945.

Ten aircraft carriers, twenty-six cruisers, and six battleships were converted into troop ships to bring soldiers home from Europe and the Pacific. The United States had more than 12 million men and women in the armed forces at the end of World War II, of whom 7.6 million were stationed abroad. Military personnel were returned to the United States in *Operation Magic Carpet.*

The rapid demobilization of American servicemen threatened to create a shortage of manpower for the occupation of Germany, Austria, and Japan. On January 4, 1946, the War Department backtracked on its previous promises of early demobilization and announced that 1.55 million eligible servicemen would be demobilized and discharged over a six-month period rather than in three months as previously announced. This announcement generated immediate protests from soldiers around the world. Four thousand soldiers in Manila demonstrated against the cancellation of a repatriation ship on Christmas 1945. The protests spread worldwide, involving tens of thousands of soldiers in Guam, Hawaii, Japan, France, Germany, Austria, India, Korea, the United States, and England.

October 27 – Saturday
Los Angeles

Hi Darling,

It's Saturday and I went to Confession. And now I am a good girl. And I love you, Bobbie.

Today was Navy Day. Los Angeles celebrated that plus Victory and together it was pretty something. There was a big parade with hundreds of planes. The planes flew in formation and spelled Army and Navy.

I saw a B-25 today flying so low you could almost see the men in it. I like B-25's. And tonight, there is a show at the Coliseum that is supposed to be the greatest the world has ever had. We've been listening to it on the radio. They are having a re-enactment of the flag-raising over Iwo Jima - of kamikaze attacks on ships and of the atom bombing. All the big stars who went into the service are on - John Garfield, Ronald Reagan, Orson Welles, Dennis Day etc. There are 100,000 people there.

Darling, Julieann and Terry are the most wonderful things that ever happened to us. They are so darling, both of them

It's night, darling, and I love you and we are getting closer together with every thought. I love you, Bob. Goodnight, darling.

Forever yours,
Mariellen

Chapter Six

1946 - 1950

My dad returned home to Los Angeles in January 1946 to quite the homecoming. He'd been gone a year and had yet to meet his baby daughter, born the past August.

Although my dad talked little about his experience fighting the war in the Pacific, he did tell us stories and anecdotes as we were growing up. We grew up singing the songs of the times - especially his Army marching songs like *The Army Goes Rolling Along*, and *Here We Go into the Wild Blue Yonder*. He was happy to be home, yet proud of what he had accomplished. He was especially honored to have been chosen to be with the 345th Air Apache unit and in the 499th Bombardment Group, called the Bats Outa' Hell where he made lifelong friends.

****

After Bob returned home, the family made several moves. He wanted to finish undergrad school and attend law school. He also joined the Air Force Reserve, on the premise that the war was over and there was little chance he would be called back up for active duty. He was intrigued with the "new B-29s", and this would give him the chance to continue to fly.

In 1947, Bob, Mariellen, and their daughters Julieann and Terry moved into a military housing in a development in Los Angeles called Rodger Young Village.

Rodger Young Village was a public housing project, established to provide temporary housing for veterans returning to the southern California area, following the end of World War II. The village was named for Rodger Wilton Young, an American infantryman killed during the war. Built in Griffith Park, Los Angeles, the village consisted of 750 Quonset huts. These temporary buildings made of corrugated steel, housed 1,500 families. At peak residence, over 5,000 people lived there.

Built in approximately two months (and over the objections of the Griffith family, who had donated the park to the city), the Village was dedicated on April 27, 1946, and closed in the mid-1950s. The Quonset hut camp met a desperate need for living space for the thousands of Californians who left the area for military duty. When these men and women returned from the war, they found that housing had been taken by the thousands who had moved to L.A. to work in plants producing war materiel.

Rodger Young Village was one of several projects the Los Angeles City Housing Authority offered to veterans and their families. For a reasonable rate they could live there while waiting for the post-war housing "boom" to counter the post-war housing "crunch." Other veterans' housing projects used military barracks and trailers, as did a settlement in Burbank, which provided travel trailers to house some of the Japanese and Japanese Americans who had been taken from their Southern California homes and sent to internment camps in other parts of the country.

Nearly all residents were young families with children (including many war brides). Each family had a half of a Quonset hut, built on concrete slab floors. The living space consisted of two bedrooms, a bath, a kitchen with an icebox (not a refrigerator), and a den.

Bob with Terry and Julieann at Roger Young Village 1946

"The Village," as it was known, had a market, hardware store, milk and diaper delivery, drug store, a theater, and other amenities commonly found in small towns. Residents planted lawns and gardens and were encouraged to make their surroundings as homelike as possible.

Few families had telephones, relying instead on phone booths located about 100 feet apart. When a phone call would come in, those closest at the moment would answer, and the neighborhood children would run to see who the call was for, then pass the word to that person. Rodger Young Village was, for a time, the most diverse community in southern California, as veterans of all races and all branches of the military lived there. This caused problems in some nearby restaurants, which were practicing de facto racial segregation, as next-hut neighbors went to dine together. The influence of Village residents helped end segregation in a number of establishments in Southern California.

Bob and Mariellen loved the years they lived there. There were many happy times as they navigated their life as a married couple, together at last. In 1948 their third child was born, a long-awaited son, and they named him James Patrick.

Always in a leadership role, my dad became Mayor of Rodger Young Village, and both he and my mom were active in the local politics as well as in their church.

Bob as Mayor of Rodger Young Village

Chapter Seven

1951-1953 - Korea

Much to my mother's dismay, my father's Air Force Reserve unit was one of the first to be called up for the Korean War. They now had three children and another on the way. The girls were five and six, and Jimmy was turning three. The kids knew and loved their dad and didn't want him to leave. This would be a much different "wartime" experience for both my mom and my dad.

The family moved to Texas in April 1951, for Bob's continued training. In the summer of 1951, my father, now a first lieutenant, was sent to Korea.

My mother stayed behind with the kids in Texas. She was again pregnant, and once again, my parents were forced to communicate across thousands of miles only through their letters.

****

After Japan surrendered to the Allies in 1945, the Korean peninsula was split into two zones of occupation – the U.S. controlled South Korea and the Soviets controlled North Korea. In 1948, amid growing Cold War tensions between Moscow and Washington, two separate governments were established in Pyongyang and Seoul.

When the North Koreans crossed the 38th parallel into South Korea on June 25th, 1950, the U.S. Army, along with the other military services, found itself ill-prepared to resist. Readiness was at a low level and when the war erupted, many combat, and service support units stood at a quarter or less of their enlisted strength. The most crucial problems were manpower and mobilization.

Between August 1950 and September 1951, over 500 miscellaneous units of the Reserve, totaling some 5,370 officers and 28,850 enlisted men, received orders to return to active duty to round out existing active Army divisions. Insufficient funds and low recruiting rates hampered the organization of all Reserve units to full strength, which would have required twenty-five times the officers and enlisted men.

The Korean War or Korean Conflict, is often referred to as “The Forgotten War” or "The Unknown War." This was due to the lack of public attention it received both during and after the war. Yet it was a brutal conflict. The U.S. suffered 33,651 battle deaths and 20,617 non-battle deaths. There were also 103,284 wounded, and 8,207 missing in action. Over 5,000 Americans were prisoners of war.

The Korean War was the first test of the United Nations’ determination to stand against tyranny in all its forms. Twenty-one nations joined with the United States to turn back blatant aggression and halt the wave of Communism.

The United Nations Command (UNC) provided the core military and strategic direction for the anti-Communist war effort in Korea. The United States provided the high command for the UNC as well as the vast majority of the air and naval power.

My dad was sent to Korea in the spring of 1951 to set up a forward observer radar system with the Fifth Air Force. He spent time in Radar and Communications toward the end of WW ll and completed intense and secret radar training in Texas before leaving for Korea.

In our family, he was considered a hero for his role in setting up the radar in Korea. His expertise and work earned him the rank of Captain and a Silver Star. Forward air operations and radar were part of communications and required a top-secret clearance rating.

****

Summer 1951

Denison, Texas

Darling,

Hi - hi. What are you doing? It's about 10:00 p.m. here. I have the sprinkler on the lawn - the dishes in the sink and I just finished cutting Jimmy's hair. Yes - isn't that terrible? Well, gosh - it was so long, and I hadn't had a chance before - so we started about 8:30. I thought it would take about 15 minutes. He was so good. It looks pretty good though. We'll take a picture of it.

Oh, guess what we did today? Oh Bob! The market had a big thing for the kids - all the little people got ice cream- and what fun. Julieann and Terry are so busy. They have been hammering. I'm going to let them pound up that box in the back.

Bob, when you come back, let's take some dancing lessons, okay?

Darling, we say the Rosary every night for you. Bob, I'm going to be on the edge of my chair until you get out of Korea. It seems like a powder keg just ready to go. Are you as uneasy as I am here? Honey - I love you.

Goodnight

Mariellen

Mariellen, the kids, and Bob before he was shipped out to Korea

My older brother Jimmy, remembers living in Denison, Texas, near the Red River.

"Our neighbor there was Mrs. Hood. She used to make the best biscuits that I could bring home, but our dog Boots ate them on more than one occasion. Dad took me, Julie and Terry fishing on the Red River. We caught several boots and shoes...Once when we were driving out to the base we saw a car on fire. Dad stopped and helped put the fire out. Another time, there was a party at our house and we found a tarantula. The kids thought this was great! But then someone's dad (not ours) stomped on it to our vast disappointment."

August 1951
Pusan, South Korea

My Darling Beautiful,

It's late, quiet, lonesome. I tried to sleep - read for hours it seemed, but no good. I wanta talk to you - The guys are all asleep - I'm sorta sneaking one late talk in - dim light - but real nice when I'm with you.

The radio a while ago was playing songs - dancing music and very romantic stuff. I could just imagine us - waltzing, doing the New Yorker stuff. After we take some lessons together, like we plan, I guess we can even do Sambas - you're very easy to dance with and hold close - very romantic.

I remember the times we danced at the Village - they are very precious memories - I'm sure we were the most handsome couple in the hall - well you were the loveliest and most beautiful.

I guess I danced about par for my whole actions - but if we take lessons together we can really show 'em - can't we?

You know we should go to a movie when I get back - a drive-in I mean - just the two of us - so we can enjoy the show - and your lips will taste like popcorn and salt. Your hair will be against my cheek - I can smell the freshness and feel the closeness of you - Is it a date?

You know what I'd like to do - after a good(?) night sleep - with you - just sit and have coffee and look at you.

Then after a big dinner of fried chicken and mashed potatoes I'd like to read the Sunday papers and then with your head in my lap, I'd like to listen to Amos and Andy.

But mostly I just want to be with you - my mind and dreams race along at about one thousand miles per hour. How we'll look when we go walking and when we go swimming and riding and where we'll eat steak and how I'll order for us - I'll teach you to make martinis for our own bar and during the hot days we'll drink beer - ok?

I guess I'll have to go and get my hair cut tomorrow - it's pretty long and in the compound here, they cut it for only

25 cents - course it's a real two-bit haircut - but cool -

I guess I better stop - it's late and the light might bother the kids - the younger fellows here -

Love,

Bob

After setting up the forward observer radar station for the Fifth Air Force in Pusan, South Korea, Bob was sent back to Texas for continued training. While there, he earned his "celestial wings," making him eligible to fly B-29 bombers at night.

He was back in the States for only a couple of months when he was again sent to Seoul, South Korea. As a pilot, navigator and radar specialist, he worked on improving both radar and short-range navigation. To cope with the Communist switch to night operations, better bombing techniques were developed.

The U.S. Air Force was tasked with supplying trained fighter pilots as forward air controllers (FACs), with the Army supplying equipment and personnel.

"Americans in 1950 rediscovered something that since Hiroshima they had forgotten: you may fly over a land forever; you may bomb it, atomize it, pulverize it, and wipe it clean of life– but if you desire to defend it, protect it, and keep it for civilization, you must do this on the ground the way the Roman legions did, by putting young men into the mud."

T. R. Fehrenbach, This Kind of War

Trench warfare was not expected as a mode of fighting in Korea. Battles such as Heartbreak Ridge lasted a full month from September 13th to October 15th, 1951. The battle of Pork Chop Hill went on for four months from March 23rd to July 16th, 1953. Neither of these battles were about seizing territory or defeating the enemy but were strategic operations whose purpose was to influence the negotiations to end the fighting and resolve the question of who would control Korea.

When the front lines became bogged down in trench warfare in the summer 1951, forward air control became less important. Still, close air support continued, and was sometimes used to delay missions against the Communist lines of communications.

SHORAN, an acronym for **SHO**rt **RA**nge **N**avigation, was a type of electronic navigation and bombing system that used a precision radar beacon. Developed during World War II it was first used in combat in the B-25, B-26 and B-29 bomber aircraft during the Korean War.

SHORAN used ground-based transponders to respond to interrogation signals sent from the bomber aircraft. By measuring the round-trip time, to and from one of the transponders, the distance to that ground station could be accurately determined. The aircraft flew an arcing path that kept it at a predetermined distance from one of the stations. The distance to a second station was also being measured, and when it reached a predetermined distance from that station as well, the bombs were dropped.

By the end of the Korean War, airborne forward air controllers alone were credited with flying 40,354 forward air control missions and directing airstrikes that killed an estimated 184,808 Communist troops. Tactical air was credited with inflicting about half of all Communist casualties.

Despite having agreed on a common forward air control doctrine as embodied in Field Manual 31 - 35 Air-Ground Operations, a turf war over doctrine raged between the U.S. Air Force and the U.S. Army for the entire war. Additionally, the U.S. Marine Corps maintained its own FAC operation. With no common doctrine agreed upon during the war, forward air control systems were shut down postwar in 1956.

****

While in Korea, my dad took pictures of the land and the people. He wrote on the backs of the pictures he sent home –

"Some of the girls that are employed and the little kids peering thru the fence - when you look at the kids you just wanta tear the darn fence down."

"School Children -The barbed wire surrounds restricted areas such as this compound for G.I.'s Kids just don't change – they all look alike (ours and theirs)"

After being home for only a few months, Bob returned to Korea in December 1951. With their fourth child due in just a couple of months, neither he nor Mariellen dreamed it would be well over a year before they would see each other again.

Rosemary, their fourth child, was born six weeks early, in January of 1952, just a month after Bob left for Korea. She had some early lung-related issues and had to remain in the hospital for several weeks.

February 1952
Fort Worth, Texas

Hi Darling,

Sunday, we had breakfast at about 10:30, so it isn't time for lunch and Rosemary is asleep. Soo - a few minutes.

We got up and went to 8:30 Mass - and we made it on time, too - got there about 3 minutes before the Priest came in. Rosemary has found out about strangers. And after she had been in church about 5 minutes, she saw them - Strangers! Oh! And does she express herself, and the tears just pour down her cheeks. This morning she was sleepy, so we got her quieted down, and with her thumb in her mouth, she went to sleep. She's so sweet.

After Mass, we lit a candle for you. What a <u>ceremony</u> - putting in the money, getting the match lighted, blowing it out - but the prayers are real and sincere - all the little Martins saying their prayers for their Daddy.

You know Mom and her five sisters are having a big reunion now. They are especially having it <u>without</u> their children or grandchildren - so Phyll and Bud and children - and Joan and Sid and Jim - all decided it would be wonderful to see everybody. So off they all went to Oregon.

Mom is really going to be irked. Anyway, I think it's funny. Only it will be a little rough. Everyone will be crowded already.

It's been over 100 degrees in Texas for 17 days, and today it's 108 in Dallas. The water supply in Dallas is critical.

It's nicer here in Duncanville. About 80 degrees and sunshiny.

Forever,
Mariellen

My oldest sister Julie remembers living in Duncanville. And she especially remembers their first experience with attending public school.

"Mom pulled us out FAST after Terry and I came home and told her the teachers had ended the school prayer with "and God protect us from Jews, Catholics and other agents of the devil." She said she remembers the exact words because she was so stunned to be called "agents of the devil." Julie doesn't think they were in the school for even a week.

Living in Texas, far from family and friends was just too hard for Mariellen. She moved back to Los Angeles, closer to her family and friends, in the spring of 1952 so she could have help and support raising the four kids. They moved around because of my dad's continued training, and the older kids went to several different schools. That was tough on everyone and the family was happy to be back in Los Angeles.

****

April 27, 1952
Monrovia, Ca

Darling,

It's Sunday evening - just the time you like. Drew Pearson is over - the little gang are all in bed and it's quiet.

Rosemary was christened this morning - and she didn't even whimper. After she was christened, Father Daly said we could take a couple of pictures in church to send to you. We all (Mom, Pop, Cloyd and all the children), went to Phyll and Bud's for a buffet lunch. We came home about 3:30 - was I glad to get home. They wanted me to stay and play cards, but I was so tired from getting ready for the big event that I just had to come home. Boy!! You know how it goes -I congratulate myself, tho- This morning when Terry spilled a bottle of shoe white polish on the kitchen floor, I didn't hit anyone or anything. I just stood with my eyes closed and counted to about 500. I believe it awed them more than noise.

Bob, Rosemary is just darling. She has dimples, eyelashes as long as Julie's, a cute little lopsided smile - and curly hair.The kids had a wonderful time today. Jim didn't have a nap and about 5 o'clock I found him sound asleep on the couch - bless his heart. California went on daylight saving time this morning. That's nice. Rosemary didn't wake up until 6:15 a.m. instead of 5:15.

Darling, we say the Rosary every night for you.

Mom and Pop came back from Oregon. They are about to accept the Ranch offer. Pop would make at least $225 (he's going to try for more) a month and they would get eggs, milk, butter, some meat and a house on top of it.

Boots is lying here looking at me - he's the best dog. He stays in the house all the time when we go. He is so interested in Rosemary and acts like he adores her.

It's raining again. Just sprinkling. I guess I'll go to bed. It seems so lonely and cold, I just put it off. Goodnight darling. I love you,

Mariellen XXOO

B-29 bombing targets in the daytime skies over North Korea.

Bob flew the B-29 Super fortress in the Korean war for the 5th Air Force. The Far East Air Forces (FEAF) was the command and control organization for the military engaged in combat. Its units were located in Korea and Japan. Fighter and troop carrier wings from Tactical Air Command and federalized Air National Guard units from the United States, deployed to the Far East, and reinforced FEAF units engaged in combat.

These tactical units conducted strikes on supply lines, attacked dams that irrigated North Korea's rice crops, and flew missions in close support of United Nations ground forces.

Bob was the designated flight leader on many missions.

By 1950, the B-29s had been reclassified as "medium" bombers, their long-range missions having been taken over by the B-36 and B-50. Many B-29s were retrieved from post-war (WWll) storage and refurbished.

At least sixteen B-29s were shot down over North Korea, and as many as 48 were lost in crash landings or grounded because of heavy damage. When the Korean War ended on July 27th, 1953, the B-29s had flown over 21,000 sorties (missions), with nearly 167,000 tons of bombs being dropped.

A typical B-29 carried forty 500-pound general purpose bombs. Each bomb was fitted with a delayed-action fuse, with a propeller on the bomb's nose. After the bomb was released from the B-29's bomb bay, the propeller turned and tightened a threaded rod running through the bomb's nose. The rod continued turning until it ruptured an acetone-filled vial. The nose fuse was filled with Plexiglas disks surrounding the acetone vial, and when the acetone vial was broken, the acetone began to dissolve the Plexiglas disks. This triggered the bomb's predetermined detonation time–from 1 to 144 hours. To prevent the North Koreans from easily defusing the delayed-action bombs, a small rod was connected to the end of the fuse, and any attempt to remove the fuse triggered an explosion.

The growing danger of being stalked by Russian MIGs and the large number of Communist anti-aircraft made it necessary for the B-29s to fly at night. The bombers usually flew in a stream formation with a 500-foot altitude separation, stepped up, and at three-minute intervals. North Korean anti-aircraft gunners soon began to anticipate where the bombers might fly, however, so the Americans then modified their target approach tactics. B-29 intervals were altered to between one and five minutes, and the separations between aircraft in the same bomber stream were mixed.

B-29s flew all but thirty days during the air war in Korea, dropping 167,000 tons of bombs on Communist targets– a greater bomb tonnage than had been dropped on Japan during World War II. Regardless of the many obstacles they faced, B-29 crews performed brilliantly, destroying industrial and military strategic targets in North Korea and supporting U.N. ground troops. The Far East Air Force lost 1,406 aircraft. Over 1000 men were killed and 306 wounded during the war. Total deaths of U.S. servicemen are estimated at 36,914.

The men who flew and supported the B-29s in the Far East Command were an important part of the air war over Korea, but their contribution has seldom been recognized.

****

Letters from Julie and Terry to their dad in Korea -

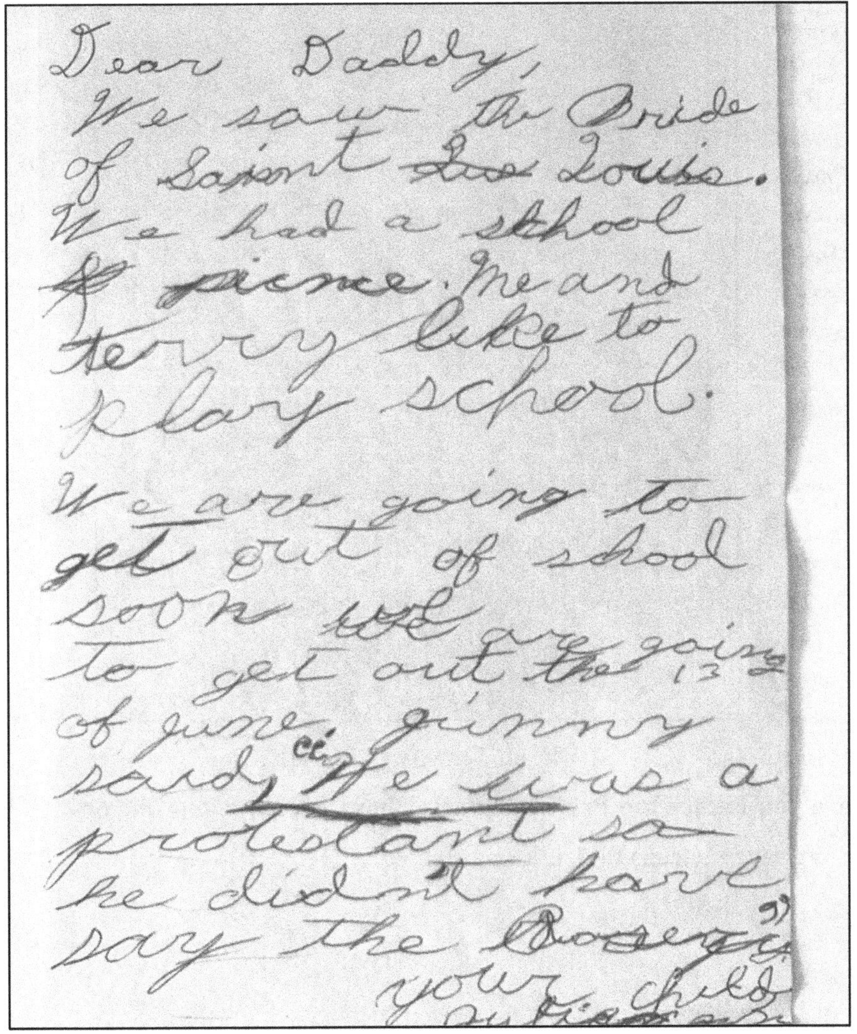

Dear Daddy,
We saw the Pride
of Saint Louis.
We had a school
picnic. Me and
terry like to
play school.
We are going to
get out of school
soon
are going
to get out the 13
of june. jimmy
said he was a
protestant so
he didn't have
say the Rosery
your child
Julieann

From Julieann age 8 years.

"Dear Daddy, We saw the Pride of Saint Louis. We had a school picnic. Me and Terry like to play school. We are going to get out of school soon. We are going to get out the 13 of June. Jimmy said he was a protestant so he didn't have to say the Rosery.

Your child, Julieann"

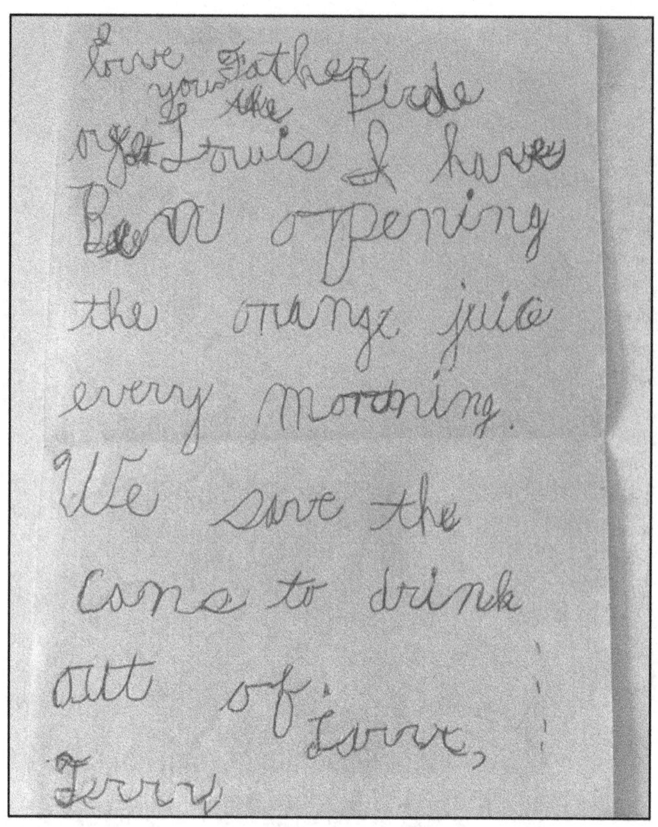

I Love you Father the Pride of Louis I have been opening the orange juice every morning. We save the cans to drink out of. Love, Terry

From Terry, Age 7 years

"I Love you Father the Pride of Louis. I have been opening the orange juice every morning. We save the cans to drink out of.

Love,

Terry"

Early June '52

Taegu, South Korea

Hi My Darling,

I love you. It's noon time. I'm going to hop out to K-2 this afternoon for a short inspection, so wanted to drop you a line now. I adore you. I've got your picture on my desk -

alone and with the little gang and Jimmy and the dog and Rosie in his arms.

I hope my dreams are reaching you - cause I love you and I want you so.

It's a real hot spell again here. My watch band burns my hand - must be pure silver - even though it only cost a buck - Maybe I've got a fortune here.

Guess I'll have to wait until tomorrow for my haircut - not that I'm going anywhere special - but it's just cooler.

Golly the morning was long and lonesome - tomorrow is little Terry's birthday. I sure hope the dolls get there in time - wish it could have been more -

I'm going to try and get ahead including the television and car if possible. I'll send you or Sears about 40 bucks for a swing set for Christmas. That seems a good gift for the consolidated gang. They can all enjoy it.

I'll be happy to see Christmas come for it'll mean only two months more and I'll be well on my way home to you - But I'll also dread it - being so far away from you.

My darling Mariellen - here's a kiss - XXOO

I love you,

Bob

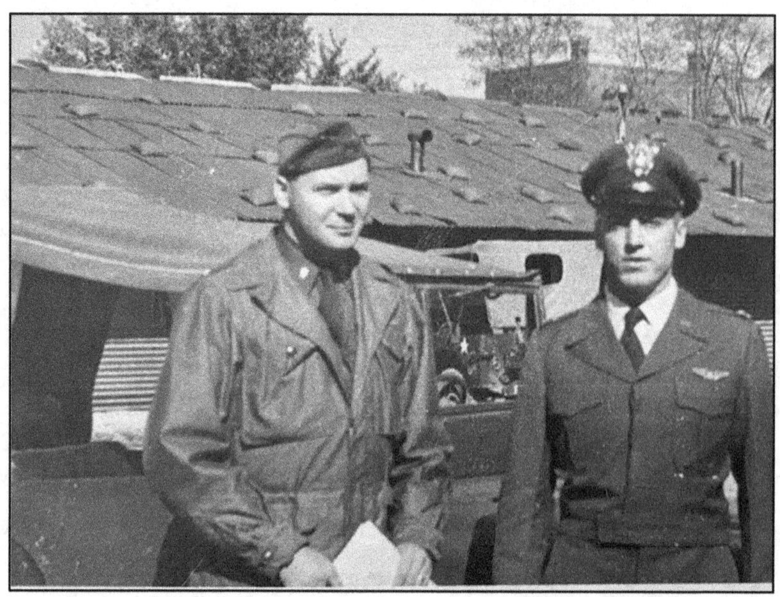

On the back of this picture Bob wrote: **"That's me to the left. My boss and I were going out to K-2 for some business. I'm not any thinner and starting my diet today. The tin roofed building behind is 5th AF Hq material building, the left wing is tactical supply (us) - the bldg. in the background is an old school used by the 28th Evacuation Hospital now."**

On the back of this photo, Bob wrote: **"A typical little gal. That's her job to tote the little one around. She hauls water and works in the field or just stands and stares. It's a great life - The wrap piece holds the baby secure. They carry them that way all day long -"**

June 1952

Monrovia, Ca.

Hi Darling,

This is pretty bad paper, but I have to write. Can you give me a hand with some of these bills? Can you send Harris and Franks, $10 - please? And the May Co. $5? Golly, I don't know what I'll do if you can't. This is what I have paid this month.

.$9 - Gas Co.

$6 - Dr. Kearns

$15 - Piano

$11.36 – Insurance

$10 - light bill

$5.50 -School

$100 – Food

$14.30 - telephone

$2.25 -Times

$80 – Rent

$37.22 - Car

$5 - Gas

The milk bill is $19.60 and Rosemary's goat milk is $7.20. So, I have $23.00 left in the bank. That's all. I'm kinda afraid.

Oh honey, I just have to get by on it. I think I can though. I really do. I have scads of food. Oh honey. I need you so much - Next month won't be quite as bad. Next month, next month. Oh darling, can you wait for your Father's Day present? Darn, darn! Please love me Bobby.

I don't know what I'm doing without you.

Yours,

Mariellen

"The Little Gang "

Wednesday – noon, July 1952

Monrovia, Ca

Hi Darling,

It's a hot afternoon - the girls just got up from a rest to go out and play in the plastic swimming pool. If they weren't brown before, they will be soon.

We took Rosemary to the doctor yesterday. She weighs 15 lbs. 11 ounces and is 25 ½ inches long. She has grown 8 ½ inches. You'd think we fertilized her or something (that wasn't meant to sound bad). How can they grow that fast?

So, you enjoyed our long talks, hmm? As I remember them, they were a monologue, with you obviously wishing you were someplace else. My gladiolus are nearly in bloom. They have long stems of buds.

I wish I had a television set for the Republican National Convention. That is something I'd really like to see. Yesterday, we went to see some kids who used to live in Colorado. I've known both of them and their families all my life. And the girl was named after mom. It was a lot of fun. Julieann really got a kick out of it - she listened to every minute of our conversation.

I miss you so in the evening. It would be so much fun to have someone for bridge - or go to the drive-in - or a game of tennis. This is evening now, 6:15 and we are through with dinner. I'm doing better. And I have to go do the dishes.

So, bye-bye darling.

I love you.

Yours - Mariellen

The 1952 Republican National Convention was the first political convention to be televised live, coast-to-coast. It was held at the International Amphitheatre in Chicago, Illinois, from July 7th - 11th. The popular General and war hero, Dwight D. Eisenhower of New York, was nominated for president. The Republican platform pledged to end the unpopular war in Korea, supported the development of nuclear weapons as a deterrence strategy, and promised to fire all "the loafers, incompetents, and unnecessary employees" at the State Department. Their platform also condemned the past administration's economic policies, opposed "discrimination against race, religion or national origin" and supported "Federal action toward the elimination of lynching." The Republican party also pledged to bring an end to Communist subversion in the United States.

At the beginning of World War II, marriage rates skyrocketed. With quick marriages came rising divorce rates. By 1946, one in four marriages ended in divorce (Mintz & Kellogg, 1988). The spike in divorce rates had many possible causes, the most obvious being a lack of foundation in the marriage.

My parents married young and had known each other for only a little over six months. My dad was gone for much of the first ten years of their marriage, either training or overseas, during WWll and the Korean War. During this time, my mother had four children and raised them for months at a time, alone.

During WWll, she was in the company of many women whose husbands were overseas. But during the Korean War, support on the local and national level was not as forthcoming. My mother felt all the stresses that come from single parenting while worrying about her husband who was away at war and flying dangerous missions. Communication was limited to letters (often delayed) and occasional calls home.

The frustration she felt in being alone began to come through in her letters. She must have felt helpless when she wrote about not having enough money for bills. With Bob so far away she had few resources to rely on. Being proud and independent were qualities my mom processed. She knew these were her children and she chose this life. So, she would accept that responsibility and do the best she could.

The Korean War is often called the "Forgotten War" because of the lack of public attention it received both during and after the war, compared to the global scale of WWII. It was first coined the "forgotten war" since October 1951 when U.S. News & World Report gave it that title. Americans did not so much forget the Korean War as never thought about it at all. When it first broke out, people worried that American involvement would usher in the same type of rationing and full mobilization like the Second World War. That didn't occur, and within a few months, most Americans turned back to their own lives, ignoring the conflict raging half a world away.

August 1952

Taegu, South Korea

My Darling,

My own Mariellen, how I miss you.

It's a warm sultry day yet writing this I'm cold with fear. My stomach is sick and knotted, my mouth is dry - Mariellen, please write.

Today they had an extra big mail load. All the odd mail from Saturday on, that had been held up at Guam and Japan due to rains. Everyone got at least 3 letters, some of the guys got 5. I didn't get one -

Over here the last chance I have of holding on to you and trying to win you back is our letters. When that's gone, all I can reach you with is dreams - don't go that far away - darling please - I know that I've made you feel out of the game. I didn't want to, just was a weak fool - but now that's over - I found I could be a man and so became one. Our love was great enough to see how dumb I was and gave me the courage and strength I needed to straighten out.

I pray it's enough to hold us now - punish me if you wish, 'cause I deserve it for hurting you, but don't make it long. Please my darling.

The fear of being alone is common to all men, and easy to feel over here, so far from everything and so close to nothing but the cold deadly fear of being alone from the loss of someone you loved because of some dumb, foolish and stupid way you acted and now deeply regret because you understand - That fear is more than I ever knew was possible. My dreams are full of things I want to say - to make up for - full of laughter and even sometimes losing together - but always as one - my dreams are of us.

I couldn't imagine you and I as separate people. There are no dreams, no life, no future there.

Give our dreams a chance to be reality, please darling. Let me have a chance to show you the happiness I've cheated you out of. Let me come home to you.

Take my heart and love and the dreams we built together - for our lives together and give me the life, courage and dreams to carry on for the remaining months over here.

To not have your love, and trust and hope - to know that my heart isn't with yours - is like living in a dark hole - in a world all alone where silence reigns - like being dead but able to feel pain.

I get all mixed up with words and confused and lost when I get scared. Afraid of losing you - If I could do it real logically or like a movie hero, I wouldn't be so frightened.

But here, where I can't put my arms about you, or my lips next to your cheek I can only hope you'll look into my heart and see the love and sincerity that's there. Know in your heart that I'll never abuse your trust again and will devote the rest of my life to making all your - our - dreams come true -

Darling please don't go away - I love you,

Bob

Monday, Sept. 8th, '52
Los Angeles, Ca.

Hi Honey,

Pretty quickly you'll be getting pictures on the back of your letters from the kids.

We went to the "Father Sullivan picnic" yesterday. Practically everyone got there. The Davis's, O'Hare's, Sullivan's, Range's, Sacco's. Cleary's, the Russo's, Bradley's, Cochranes, Calhan's, and McNulty's. It was a lot of fun. Everyone just gabbed. Ralph is a distributor for Wonder Bread - he's just the same - a nice guy and the life of the party. Cleary's have a baby due any day (4th), The Ranges have 6 children. Sullivan's have 4. The Bradley's have a swishy convertible. The Roy's have a new Dodge. The Shannon's - remember them - have 5 children and a station wagon. Everyone had to keep a sharp watch on their children in mortal fear that one of the Courtney boys (from the 1 ½ year old to the biggest) would get hold of them.

Bob, don't act dumb with me darling. Remember me - I know you. Don't ask me if I'm mad honey. I haven't started this off very well - dumb isn't a good word. When you get to be our age you begin to appreciate the reasons God instituted matrimony, hmm? So many things come and go so fast. It is a wonderful thing to have a companion, a lover who has shared it and the security of facing the unknown. You didn't take your opportunity and you've lost it forever.

There are so many mysterious things - joy so great, it's pain. You've lost 10 years of pure beauty that can't ever be regained or replaced. Because every person has beauty in them, no matter who they are - and the one who loves them is rewarded with it. A person who hasn't touched it is sad, but for a person to have a chance and not take it - it is a tragic thing. To have it shining there and take fool's gold instead.

You are right in saying to look ahead and I know you are. Only when I don't write, don't think I'm mad. Just struggling to keep my perspective. And honey when you read this, don't just read the flat paper. It's so deep in my heart. The ache too.

Goodnight Bob, I love you – Mariellen

September 1952

South Korea

Darling,

How can I say what I want to? How can I tell you of my fears and love, so you can understand? With tears in my eyes, I'm asking you Mariellen to please write - tell me you understand how I want you and how deep my love is - how right it is. Please write and tell me you know I'll love you honestly and devotedly all the rest of our lives.

Please don't go away - You've no idea how lonely and terrible it is without you - mostly the fear of losing you.

Please write, my darling wonderful wife - please - please tell me you want me to come back - please.

I love you,

Bob

Monday - 15th, '52

Los Angeles

Bobbie Darling,

All right darling - let's go on from here. You have my love and trust. Bob, you do have the right to them - you're no ordinary guy, you know. Oh darling - I read your letters - crying until I can hardly see. There is nothing I want more than to give you my love. Honey, they aren't hard to give. So, will this do to go on - until you get home? And I'll trust you all right? Oh Bobbie, I love you, I love you. Only don't hurt me and don't leave me.

Right now, what I really want is for you to come home. In one piece, so we can be together. The world is such a screwy place now, that I'll feel better when we get closer.

The girls started back to school this morning. We live closer now. About three minutes in the car. Five to ten minutes walking. About four to five blocks.

Julieann had a rough time today. She got an infection in a blister on her hand. She had to be given anesthetic and have it lanced - a double shot of penicillin and another one tomorrow. Then she has to have it dressed again on Wednesday. It looked ugly - her hand was swollen to nearly twice its size. I was afraid she had blood poisoning. I think she was on the verge. If I had noticed it sooner - but she doesn't complain and by the time she showed it to me last night, it was already terribly swollen. Golly.

Mom and Pop sent all four of the little people each two pairs of pajamas - really nice ones.

I love you.
Forever yours,
Mariellen

The pain in both their voices is easy to hear. And hard to think about. Though my parents didn't talk about this "bump" in the road. We wonder now what could have happened.

It could be that letters are missing. Or simply that it was a lack of communication, intentional or not. Or perhaps it was something bigger, something more serious.

I can say this - my father made good on his promise. Letters are like a promissory note. A written receipt, signed, sealed, and delivered. A phone call can offer empty words, but a letter is a contract. My dad devoted himself to my mom for the rest of their lives. And she to him. They never missed an opportunity to say "I love you" to each other. They never denied each other a hug or embrace.

If these letters didn't exist, we (their children), would never have guessed at the hard times and rough patches in their marriage. I believe that is what makes this so real. These are real letters, a true story. They speak frankly and honestly of hardships and lessons learned, either away at war or on the home front.

Forgiveness. The strength it must have taken my mom to forgive my dad is almost unimaginable. He had been gone almost a year when she received this letter. She was raising four children alone. Whatever did happen, her heart didn't harden. She found a resiliency perhaps she didn't even know she had and moved on with her life.

My mother was a converted Catholic. When she met my dad, she didn't belong to any church or congregation. My dad was a devout Catholic, and she embraced his religion. She was baptized, confirmed, and married all within the first year they were together. From that time on, she was devoted to her faith. She said the Rosary daily. She prayed a Novena anytime she felt the need for intervention. She went to Mass daily when she could.

My mother had a grace about her that allowed her to love and to forgive. She believed in divine intervention and compassion and mercy. Growing up, we often had people at our dinner table that I didn't know: pregnant teen-age girls, immigrants, and those down on their luck. I believe her faith kept her going and held her up during the years my dad was overseas.

Mariellen's parents had recently moved from Los Angeles to a ranch in Oregon. A letter to Mariellen (and Bob) from her mother

October '52

Junction City, Or.

My Dear Ones,

I hope you two will not get too discouraged. I believe that God blesses the dreamers and hopeful ones. You two have big ideas and big dreams and high hopes. Keep on having them. Don't be afraid - you haven't been - now because things are a bit tough - you must still retain your hopes and plans. Bob makes me so mad when he says he is a heel. He could never be that. He is a grand person and you Mariellen - are a girl to inspire hope and ambition. You don't need to tell me that you are not complaining - you never do. Okay now, are your chins up? Well that's swell. My faith in the two of you is unbounding.

I am anxiously awaiting a letter from you. I do worry about the girls. It took so long for your letters to arrive. Hope it doesn't take as long for mine to get to you. Shall I send your package or wait? I am a lazy gal - I didn't get up until 10:00 a.m. Had a little set back. I have to take it pretty easy. Am getting better. I must iron today - then I am going to the beach to be alone for two weeks. I don't have too much to do - only can't do it for a little while. It won't bother me at all - you all being here - please believe me. You can go and take care of your things and everything will be grand. Must close now and I do hope I hear from you soon. We are looking forward to seeing you. Please let me know (how the babies) are.

Much Love,

Mother

My dad rarely talked about his experiences during WWll. In his later years, as he was going through his belongings, he explained pictures, medals, honors, and things he had saved. As little as he spoke of WWll, he never spoke at all about Korea. The only thing he ever said was that in the winter, he was always cold. All the time. The coldest he'd ever been.

Dean Acheson, who served as Secretary of State, once said of Korea:

"If the best minds in the world set out to find us the worst possible location in the world to fight this damnable war, the unanimous choice would have been Korea."

G.I.s wanted to go home. Korea's frigid winters, blistering summers, and endless ridgelines made serving there quite miserable.

The winter of 1950 started in the middle of November in Korea. American troops did not have the proper gear to guard against the intense Siberian cold. Some wrapped towels around their heads to protect their ears. They doubled or even tripled the layers of clothing they wore. Even with the extra protection, soldiers lost fingers, toes, and ears to frostbite. In artillery units, men poured gasoline into empty 105mm shell casings to be used as heaters. Others simply poured the gasoline directly into the dirt, then lit the ground on fire. Despite rules forbidding them, most troops built small campfires from anything they could get their hands on, including the bundles of rice straw the Koreans left next to rice paddies. When enemy troops began booby-trapping the bundles with grenades, American soldiers were reminded that staying warm in a war zone was a deadly challenge.

The U.S. troop casualties from The Battle at Chosin Reservoir in the winter of 1950 were painfully high. The estimated 18,000 casualties included 7,998 killed or missing in action. More than 5,000 were wounded. With temperatures as low as −36 °F, another 8,000 suffered from frostbite. American forces were surrounded, vastly outnumbered, and faced mass slaughter in the brutally cold mountains near the Chinese border. Ultimately, some American units took the brunt of the attack, allowing others to escape on a hard-fought 70-mile march to the coast.

October 1952
Taegu, South Korea

My Darling Mariellen,

It's really blowing a storm up here - these tin huts are creaking and straining. It rained all night and most of the day. What weather. Cold too - the 'ole fall is coming fast, however I expect some more hot weather this month.

The few trees have just started to get ready for fall. I'm glad to see winter come, for as they say, "If Winter comes, can Spring be far behind" and can you be far away.

The pictures were real terrific. I can't tell you how happy they made me. The day brightened about 1 million candlepower. Your picture was the best ever - I sure am lucky to have you - golly, you are truly beautiful. So nice, so fresh and clean - so much my wife - so much a gal to believe in and work forever for.

Due to foul weather the business at hand has been rather slow - but it's still too fast for me. Not that I'm lazy, but the excessive amount of work doesn't give me enough time for dreaming of you - and that is my priority job in this theatre.

We are writing our monthly history. It's surprising how much and how little you do each month.

Tell Julieann I really wasn't too worried about the washing machine taking my place - just the delivery man and the salesmen. Yes Julie is cute, nearly as lovely as her mommy.

Gee, I miss you. Oh honey, renew your trust - you have it deep in your heart. Please dig down and get it again. All last night I dreamed of us together. It's a wonderful thought and I'm devoted to your life forever. Some guys think in terms of money - manpower and such. I think in terms of you. I love you. The pictures of the house look wonderful. It's painted dark green huh? You know, you have never told me a word about it. How you got it - what it looks like - bedrooms, fireplace?

My darling, I don't know what to say about the trip north. It's going to be awfully lonesome there alone. And the kids would have so much fun in the snow and so would you. Can you take the train most of the way? I sure can't see a long bus ride - not from L.A.

What worries me most is can you manage the little gang all alone. If it were me, I wouldn't go cause I can't stand to be with my relatives for long in close quarters anyhow - but yours are different. You do what you want dearest. The trip, the change, the whole thing would be grand for you and the kids - but the trip home, and all the work to catch up would be tough - and don't you dare meet any kind of helpful wolves or handsome bus drivers.

My dearest, my heart is yours, but I worry all the time that somehow you may be found out by another who has his heart there and - I know it's silly but I love you so much - You have my whole heart and love. I love you,

I love you, I love you,

Forever, Bob

Tuesday, November 1952
Los Angeles

Hi Sugar,

No, the house isn't green. You must get about half of my letters. I've told you at least twice about the house. I hate to think about all those letters going to waste. All those stamps - and I think you missed out on one set of pictures.

To get back to the house. It's not quite as pretty as it looks. It's kind of a chocolate brown - not bad tho. Bobby- really didn't you know how I got the house? One of those miracles. I came home from the clinic with that awful tooth and had an eviction notice for three weeks waiting for me. Oh!

I called up Fr. Martin and asked him if he knew of anything. He is a wonderful man, Bob. He found this house and gave me the money - $50 - to pay the rent for the last half of the month. No strings. Everyone in the Parish loves him - really. None of the gushy stuff. I'm going to send $10 a month for collection anyway - but not to pay it back - because we should have done it anyway. Only I wish you might send him a thank you note to the Church of the Annunciation Parish, Arcadia, Calif. I don't know what I would have done. He told me he had the house and I called about it. But it was double rent and when Father called back to see if I got it, I told him I couldn't take it. And when I told him I just didn't have the reserve, he said "Well, you have to have a house" and told me to go ahead and take it. I was in such a daze, that I went right ahead. And he brought me $50. He's a good man - sharp too - but a real man of God. From Brooklyn, bless him.

If you knew how bad the darned tooth was - you'd see what a nightmare those weeks were - the oral surgeon up here took 5 stitches in one cut where the old boy's chisel slipped. And at the end of two weeks when the doctor took the packing out, one side of the molar was open to the air from the top to the bottom of the root. You could see nearly a half inch of bare bone between the two teeth. He was a good doc tho. It's nearly all filled up now with flesh.

Oh! And tonight, I've got the curse. I'm tired. Gosh - isn't it all awful? I think I'll drink a can of beer. Do you think I might have good dreams? Of you?

I'm sorry the last two letters didn't get to you.

Oh Bob, I'm so tired and there is so much to do. Too much. I need you.

Goodnight honey,

I love you

Yours,

Mariellen

****

Stories from surviving Korean POWs were fraught with emotion and horror. These men endured cruel beatings, were placed in solitary confinement, and denied food and water.

The captors led their prisoners on horrific death marches. The POW's walked excruciatingly long distances with very little food and water. Civilians threw stones at them from the side of the road. If a prisoner collapsed or could not continue, he was shot, clubbed, or bayoneted to death. Men died of starvation and dehydration each day. Prisoners were often kept in "sweat boxes" that were roughly the size of a casket. Others recalled being kept in cages or caves.

Forty-three percent of American POWs died in captivity. Chinese and North Korean captors removed prisoners who they thought were resisting the pro-Communist message, or who seemed like they might revolt. They singled out pilots and officers. Many of those separated were taken away and shot.

In what was called "Operation Glory" after the Korean Armistice in 1954, North Korea returned the remains of more than 3,000 Americans.

From 1990 to 1994, North Korea uncovered and returned 208 boxes of remains. The United States Department of Defense's scientists estimate that the remains of as many as 400 people could be held in these boxes. By 2018, 182 victims had been identified.

In the Singapore Summit in 2018, North Korea committed again to recovering POW/MIA remains. On July 27th, 2018, North Korea handed over 55 more boxes. The remains were saluted in a ceremony honoring the U.S. soldiers. The North Korean authorities reported to the U.S. Defense POW/MIA Accounting Agency that they couldn't be sure how many individuals were represented in the 55 boxes. There was only one dog tag among the remains. Other servicemen may be identified through matching DNA, chest X-rays, and dental records. Twenty of the boxes were retrieved from the site of the *Battle of Unsan*, and thirty-five boxes from the site of the *Battle of Chosin Reservoir.* Also, inside were boots, canteens, and other equipment.

By October 2019, it was reported that 35-40 servicemen had been identified from the remains in the 55 boxes. After the failure of the Hanoi Summit in February 2019, the U.S. suspended the program.

As of December 2018, almost 8,000 U.S. military personnel who fought in the Korean War remain unaccounted for. This includes those still captive or missing at the conclusion of the war, or those killed in action and whose remains have not been located, recovered, and identified. The U.S. military estimates that 5,300 of these service members were lost in North Korea.

Thirty Air Force men who had been declared missing were eventually returned to military control, and 214 POWs were repatriated under the terms of the armistice agreement, while thirty-five men were still in Communist captivity in June 1954. A total of 7,245 American soldiers and airmen were captured by the Chinese and North Koreans. Of these American POWs, approximately 2,806 died in captivity.

I wish now I could ask my dad about his experiences in Korea, and how he managed to deal with all the fallout that comes after service. I guess I'll never know, but based on his accomplishments following the two wars, his quiet determination to move on with his life and family, proved to be a good one.

Thanksgiving 1952

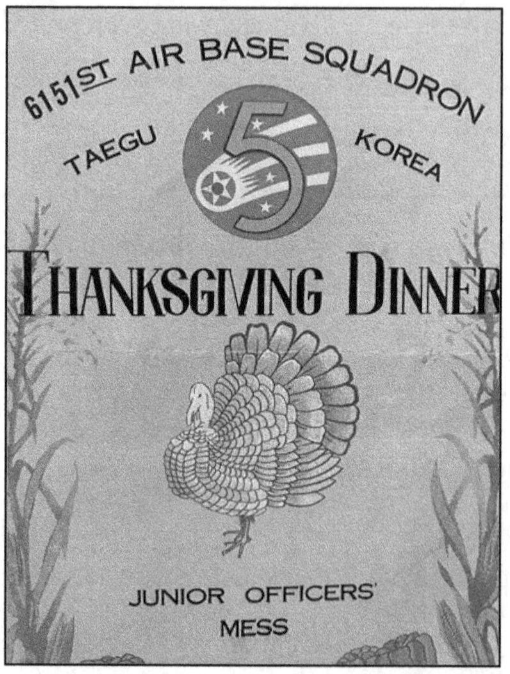

Bob spent Thanksgiving at the 6151st Air Base in Taegu, Korea.

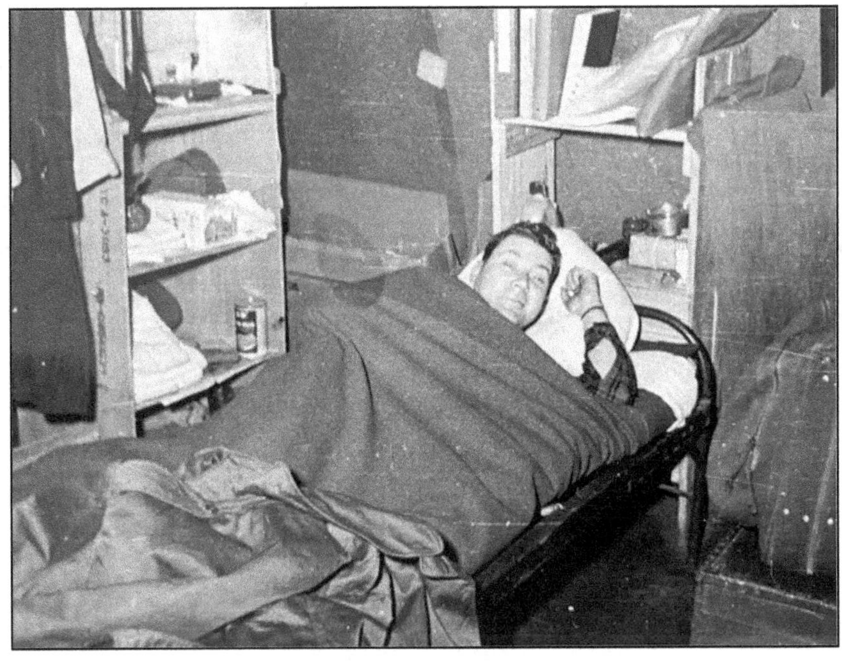

Bob in his bunk

At home in Los Angeles, Mariellen spent Thanksgiving with her four children and extended family. A typical Thanksgiving dinner for ten, cost $6.52. Dwight Eisenhower had just been elected president, and the transistor radio and the polio vaccine were developed.

November 1952
Los Angeles, Ca.

Bob Darling,

We went to mail some letters this evening. Many people have their trees up and homes decorated. It seems like there are more beautiful stories and songs on the radio than ever before.

You may get a box of Christmas cookies soon - the little people are going to spend Saturday baking cookies in every shape and form with silver balls - red, blue, and green decorations. The kitchen will be warm and spicy - the whole house will smell delicious. And when you take a bite - you won't just be getting a taste of a warm bright home, but also happy little hearts and lots of love all reaching out to you. And love reaching out to you from me - and warmth - and fun - mmm!

Rosemary looks wonderful - and she really is adorable - oh she's darling! She has the cutest smile. Oh wait 'til you see her. She sleeps all night, every night. She's as good as gold.

Honey, when I see people together - husbands and wives - I really miss you then.

I love you,
Mariellen

Korea - Christmas
December 25, 1952

Merry Christmas - Dearest - I love you

Back at the grind all day. This Air Force is a wonderful deal - where else can you get the opportunity to work on days like Christmas and such - and be so far away from your family and loved ones.

I opened your presents last night - Golly you are wonderful- the pictures of the little gang and you are the most wonderful present I could ever get. Julie sure looks lovely. Like a dream fairy. I remember when you used to call her "punkin' seed." She's very beautiful. And Terry - she's like a little Angel out of Heaven itself, but earthy enough to be the most precious thing on earth - in the world. Little Jimmy - is really our little guy. He always looks like he is about ready to come out with one of his famous sayings.

And the little stranger - she looks like a square headed Dutchman - but really very beautiful - and why not? The mother of those wonderful kids is the lovely lady in the picture. Your look - your smile - the way you are sitting and the tilt of your head. I love each thing about you - A guy with a family like that has been five times blessed by God. I knelt and thanked him from my whole heart in church - for you - for us this coming year.

About now you are being awakened by the little guys who will be eager to see what Santa has left. The thought of that scene brings a smile to my lips -

The fruitcake was wonderful too - it was still moist, and all the guys really raved. You are a good cook darling. The ties were just right - even too good in quality - every guy was delighted, and your ears should burn with praise - you're a real dream gal - I love you. That was a smart idea to pack the food in popcorn - it wasn't busted at all. The pickles were out of this world. We had a tasty snack. I've forgotten how good kosher food tasted.

But mostly thanks for you - my wife,my gal,
my life.
Bob

Christmas for Bob was spent in Korea at the 6151st Air Base in Taegu, just as he had for Thanksgiving.

The newspaper *Stars and Stripes,* dated January 5, 1953, details important phases of Korean operations in 1952. The Eighth Army review called it a deadlock with the boundary line virtually unchanged since November 1951. Yet approximately 12,600 American lives were lost that year.

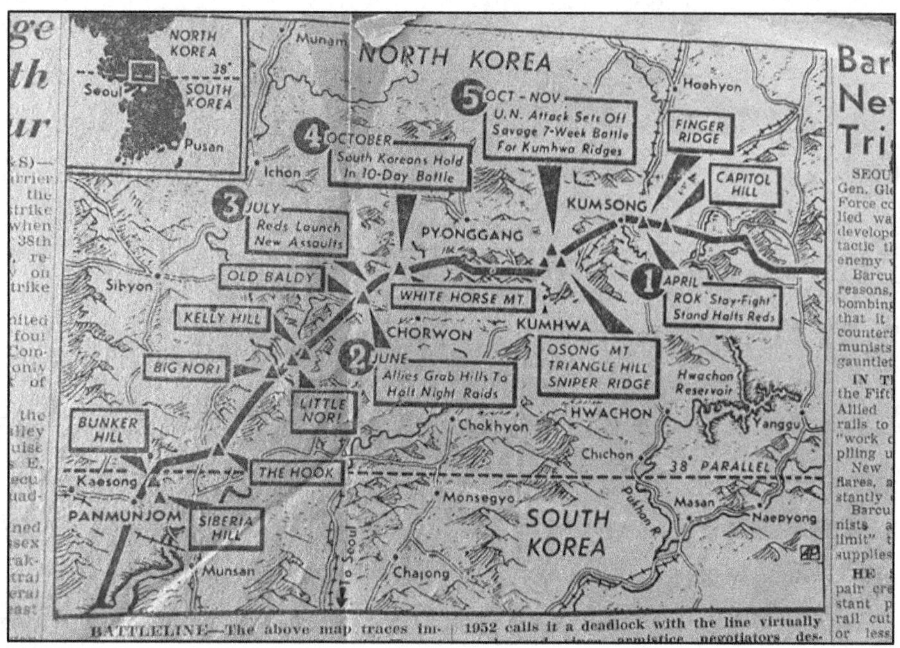

Copy of newspaper my father saved

12 Jan '53
South Korea

My Dearest Mariellen,

I love you - Brrr - the temperature must have dropped nearly 700 degrees since last night. No snow, but it's cloudy and dark and cold.

Had a very busy day - the boss left for Japan early this morning and I went to a meeting with the ROK (Republic of Korea) Air Force people all day. Very interesting - met several ROK Colonels and General Kim. We were actually setting up their authorizations for a couple of wings - they sure are eager people at times. The Colonel and General had been to school in the States and were pretty sharp.

I'm sure fed up with the military - I'm not bragging - but I just used common sense and set up some political levels for their groups and the dumb fools from the Air Force would have really botched things up if they had a chance. Not that they are dumb - particularly - just stupid and pushed into high level command jobs without the background and knowledge required.

No more info on our departure dates yet but we are sweating it out. I love you - The next two weeks will be very busy because it's that time of year - and I'm glad for it - makes the time go faster.

Gee I love you. I'd sure like to cover up against you tonight. I love you. Darling, we will have such a wonderful life together - courage and love and understanding - those are the things that we have, Golly, I love you.

The wind sure is blowing - whistles right down through the cracks and really drives your heat away and your head under covers looking for you - I love you, Bob

January 1953

Los Angeles

Dearest -

Bobbie, when you're happy, you're just happy aren't you? You don't count the reasons or even notice them much. Oh darling, I miss you so. I miss making the days into our days - thinking of you coming home at night. There are a lot of things I'd like to do better when we have a home together again. Jeepers Bob, I wish I could talk to you. I need to.

I dream of you. I love you so much. To be right in your arms, close to your heart because that's the place I want to be most in the world. This doesn't seem very real, you being here.

I wonder where you are right now? How would you like to be in a big soft bed, clean and nice and have me rub your back and your neck and love you, love you, love you, love you.

Oh, Bobbie, Bobbie, I just want you to come home.

Then I'll be happy.

Forever Yours, Mariellen

Feb 1953

Taegu SK

Dearest Mariellen,

It's a beautiful day - the sun is shining in a clear blue sky - the weather is crisp and cold - the only thing wrong, and it's everything, is that I'm 6000 miles away from you. I've read and re-read your letter many times - it's the most wonderful thing I've ever seen. I'm going to save it forever. Honey, I love you.

It's not melting a bit - well maybe a little, but it's still awful cold. I packed my boots in my footlocker and now it's plenty cold on my feet. The boss went flying today so I had a little of the pressure off - actually I'm almost FIGMO* now so I don't do very much anyhow - my replacement hasn't shown up yet but I'm supposed to get out of here anyhow. The date for our reporting over at Japan has been set for 10 Feb.

Dearest, I didn't forget your birthday. I got a card and I could have gotten you a present sent by mail but this is a very important thing and I want to go to Japan and pick it out myself. My gifts to you have become a whole lot more important now - they are going to be part of you. I love you.

Boy, I wanta kiss you - all of you - and all the time. I love you. Well, by knowing the base supply officer I got myself a new blue B-4 bag* - really ritzy - oh dearest, let's go to bed - please, please, I love you.

I know you want to be able to answer this - actually any letters mailed after the 30th from you to me will stand a good chance of being returned - but I'll have the answer in my heart.

Some people just talk by telephone or letters, but you and I can communicate all day long with our hearts and all night in our dreams. Honey I love you and want you and I don't intend to settle for one minute less - you're going to have me all the way, every second and that's just the way I want you.

I love you - forever,

Bob

**** FIGMO - Fuck It Got My Orders***

***** The Officers B-4 bag is like a portable wardrobe. On the inside, there are two zippers running halfway down each side, so when the bag is laid out flat and unzipped, your uniform can be easily placed in and hung up on the brass hoop at the top.***

The Korean War Veterans Memorial is on the National Mall in Washington, D.C. The memorial commemorates the sacrifices of the 5.8 million Americans who served in the U.S. Armed Services during the three-year period of the Korean War. It consists of four parts:

<u>The Statues</u> at the Memorial are seven feet tall and represent an ethnic cross-section of America. They stand in patches of Juniper bushes and are separated by polished granite strips, which symbolize the rice paddies of Korea.

The Mural Wall has 41 panels covering 164 feet. Over 2,400 photographs of the Korean War were obtained from the National Archives. They were enhanced by computer to give a uniform lighting effect and the desired size. The mural represents the forces supporting the foot soldier and depicts Army, Navy, Marine Corps, Air Force, and Coast Guard personnel and their equipment.

The Pool of Remembrance is a reflective pool. It encircles the "Freedom Is Not Free" inscription Wall at the base of which are listed the cost of the war in terms of KIA (Killed in Action), WIA (Wounded in Action), MIA (Missing in Action), and POW (Prisoners of War). The Pool is encircled by a path bordered by benches.

The United Nations Wall is a walkway on which are engraved markers that list the 22 nations that sent troops to the United Nations efforts in the Korean War.

On July 27th, 1953, after three years of a bloody and frustrating war, the United States, the People's Republic of China, North Korea, and South Korea agreed to an armistice, bringing the Korean War to an end. A new border between North and South Korea was drawn, which gave South Korea some additional territory and demilitarized the zone between the two nations. The war cost the lives of millions of Koreans and Chinese, as well as over 36,000 Americans. In addition, 103,284 were wounded, and 8,200 were listed as missing in action, or lost or buried at sea.

****

Chapter Eight

1953 - Epilogue

My dad made it home by the end of February 1953. He met Rosemary for the first time (she was just over a year old). Though shy at first, she quickly warmed up to him as the other kids clamored for his attention. The family was together, and that was all that mattered.

He was awarded the Silver Star for his work in Forward/Ground Radar Operations. He'd been granted access to "Secret-Security Information" for the performance of officially awarded duties. His awards, medals, and citations were something he was proud of, yet never spoke about.

Soon after Bob returned from Korea, the family moved from Los Angeles to Colorado, just outside of Denver. Bob continued to serve in the Air Force Reserve until 1958, retiring as a captain. At one point during the Cold War he was asked by the military to continue in a top-secret position. This time he declined.

Three more children were born, two girls and a boy.

Now there were nine of us: seven kids and our parents. Yet it often felt like many more. We were all busy with different activities. Everyone had their own strengths and interests, and days were filled with friends, relatives, and house guests coming and going.

Life in Colorado was never dull. We lived in a big, red saltbox-style house on five acres and had horses, cows, sheep, and poultry.

1960 - The Martin Family

Back row - L to R - Rosie, Jimmy, Julie, Terry

Front row - L to R - April, Bob, Mariellen, Katy and Jack

Bob settled into a career in contracts and negotiations. With his military background and expertise in law and contracts, he was valuable at negotiating terms between private companies and the government. He worked on the Titan-Apollo project, which put the U.S. into space and became part of the pioneering space program. He often traveled to Washington, D.C., and also overseas for business.

Following the electronic and aerospace boom, the entire family of nine moved to the Bay Area in California, where Bob worked in radar and communications, then contracts and negotiations for the next twenty years. He began teaching classes in negotiations, contracts, and procurement at the local Community College then ended his career teaching contract negotiations at Stanford University until 1985.

Once in California, we lived in the redwoods. We had horses, donkeys, sheep, and chickens. Always dogs, and now always cats! Long after dinner was over, there were many lively nights around the table with debates going on. Then, the dictionary or encyclopedia would be brought out to solve issues being argued. Our house was a crazy, loving place to grow up in. Too soon, the older kids started going off to college, the Peace Corps, and the service during the Vietnam War.

My dad was a hero. Not just because he was a highly decorated military man, but more so because of his dedication to his family and his community. He was smart, loving, and involved. He served on school boards, church boards, and leadership forums. He was kind, funny and adventurous. He never bragged about his accomplishments. Instead of parading around his ribbons and medals, he was most proud of his children and family. And, the one person he loved more than anything, or anyone, was my mom.

If my father was a hero, and he was, then my mother was a hero ten-fold. She met and fell in love with a young air cadet, and for the next ten plus years, she was often alone, raising a family, living in military housing, and supporting the war effort on the home front. She was a strong woman, to go through so much alone, and she became stronger because of it. She was a remarkable mom who could do everything. She cooked, sewed, cleaned, nurtured, and loved. She encouraged all her children to be individuals with a strong sense of community and fairness. She brought culture, music, art, religion, and politics into our home. She held our family together. And she adored, above all, my dad.

Over the years, she finished school, and when the youngest was in elementary school, she began teaching Junior High English. She was a pioneer in teaching kids with learning disabilities, and that quickly became her expertise.

On July 12th, 1973, a devastating fire on the sixth floor at the National Personnel Records Center (NPRC) in St. Louis, Missouri, damaged or destroyed official military personnel files. Shortly after midnight, a fire was reported at the NPRC's military personnel records building. The fire burned out of control for 22 hours, and it took two days before firefighters were able to re-enter the building. Due to the extensive damage, investigators were never able to determine the source of the fire.

Air Force records that were destroyed on the sixth floor were for personnel that were discharged between September 25th, 1947, to January 1st, 1964, with names alphabetically after Hubbard. That group included my dad. He was notified and asked to send in any information that could help reconstruct his military files. He never did. We did eventually reestablish most of his record, but we have their letters, which are so much more valuable than a military file. All the more reason that these letters, along with all the pictures, blood chits, patches, maps, medals, and pins, are so important. They bring a tangible sense of the life he and my mom lived.

My parent's letters were cherished by both of them. From two wars, my father saved and brought home the letters he received from my mom. In turn, my mother kept his letters through multiple military moves while raising children on her own.

First-person narratives, as in letters or diaries, are considered among the most valuable sources of historical importance. They provide intimate and personal details, thoughts, emotions and experiences. Letters offer a look into everyday life— from home, to military training and combat.

During World War ll and the Korean War, mail, in the form of letters, was the sole form of communication. Letters are time capsules in envelopes. The physical pieces themselves offer much in the way of information: the paper they were written on, the handwriting or typeface, the V-mail stationery, the stamps, addresses, and the censors' marks.

Old letters are enlightening. After time and distance, it's easier to see what the person was including, maybe without realizing it.

After my dad returned home from the Korean War, the need to write letters to each other ended, yet from the moment they met, their life together had revolved around letters as the way of communicating. They shared emotions, vulnerabilities, and strengths. They spoke of ambitions and desires. They grew up together - through their letters. Imagine waiting for replies that could take up to several weeks, wondering, second guessing your last writing. From the time they met until they were together again after World War ll, they saw each other only 144 days out of almost four years.

Writing about my parents began as a way of honoring their legacy as survivors of two wars, having only love and letters to connect them. Their letters to each other brought me closer to them in a way I never imagined. In one of my mom's letters, while struggling with perspective on how she felt, she wrote: "*And honey when you read this, don't just read the flat paper. It's so deep in my heart. The ache too.*" In other words, she is asking my dad to "read between the lines" and understand what she was really trying to say, when you can communicate through letters.

Parents are the most important people in a child's life. They help us every step of the way in our growth and development. Our perspective on life, morality, and our own vision for the future begins with them.

Often, we write about our parents as a way to better know and understand them--how they acted, how they lived-- to better understand ourselves. A glimpse into their lives offers us a chance to see ourselves, our children, and maybe even our future.

I wrote about my parents through their own words and thoughts. I found it to be equally easy and hard. Easy because I wrote about two people I knew so well and loved so much. Hard because I shared details and thoughts so intimate and personal. Yet this was a story that they were proud of and shared with all of us. My mom had talked about "someday" writing this book herself. She never got the chance.

My mom was forever a letter writer. This was her final letter to my dad.

January 2005

My Darling Bob,

It's so hard without you, my friend, my husband. I'm going to try really hard, honey. God, I'm going to try.

Today, a former student is taking me to lunch. He's having a very rough time. Do you think our experience might be able to help him? You know having our own seven kids might have forced us to take responsibility we might have evaded otherwise - what do you think?

Darling, my darling. I love you so much. Help me laugh like we used to. We were so in love all our lives. I would have been in love with you in the second grade! It was always like a shock, a physical shock when we touched.

Two people in one person - we completed each other. I'm going to have to get used to ...

We had so many of the same likes and dislikes. Books!! Not necessarily the same ones, but books! Houses - the big red one and the one in the redwoods. The one in Nucla and the one in G.J. on the lake.

We both loved sports especially tennis, although compared to you, I less than gave you a game. We loved bridge and loved to play together as a team.

We loved many things together - but one thing we both loved dearly, was each other. I love you dearly. Please, please darling don't go away. You were so sweet, and so much fun. The last time I came into your room at the hospital, - our eyes met - and it was like it always has been - sparkly, laughey - like no one else was there. Oh, I love you my darling.

Hold my hand – it's pretty rocky.

CPSIA information can be obtained
at www.ICGtesting.com
Printed in the USA
LVHW060422011220
673111LV00045B/1027

9 781647 190088